CHRISTMAS

collectors edition

R&R PUBLICATIONS MARKETING PTY LTD

Published by
R&R Publications Marketing Pty Ltd
ABN 78 348 105 138

PO Box 254, Carlton North
Victoria 3054, Australia
PHONE: (61 3) 9381 2199
FAX: (61 3) 9381 2689
E-MAIL: info@randrpublications.com.au
WEBSITE: www.randrpublications.com.au
AUSTRALIA-WIDE TOLL-FREE: 1800 063 296

Christmas – Collectors Edition

PUBLISHER: Anthony Carroll
COMMISSIONING EDITOR: Neil Hargreaves
ART DIRECTOR: Neil Hargreaves
GRAPHIC DESIGNER: Elain Wei Voon Loh
SERIES DESIGNER: Elain Wei Voon Loh
FOOD PHOTOGRAPHY: Brent Parker Jones,
R&R Photostudio (www.rrphotostudio.com.au)
FOOD STYLISTS: Lee Blaylock, Sebastian Sedlak
Neil Hargreaves
RECIPE DEVELOPMENT: R&R Test Kitchen
PROOFREADER: Stephen Jones

ISBN 978-1-74022-690-5

Printed June 2008
Computer Typeset in
ITC Avant Garde Gothic
Printed in China

Contents

Introduction

It's that time of year again! The seasons change, the pace of daily life quickens, and we all know we are heading into the fun but busy time that is Christmas.

One of the most enjoyable things about Christmas is the way it can be drawn out over a period of weeks – the build-up and anticipation, including all those pre-Christmas parties, are almost as much fun as the actual day.

You'll find *Collector's Edition Christmas* an invaluable asset to help you through 'the season to be jolly', as we have assembled some heart-warming traditional favorites, some fun new ideas, and also some more casual recipes. There is even a chapter of cookies that can double as decorations for the tree – hours of fun for all the family. You will probably be the only house on the block with edible Christmas tree decorations!

Christmas is a time of sharing and inclusiveness, and this should be the same when it comes to the Christmas meal, so don't forget those who may have special dietary requirements. Also, generally healthy alternatives are never a bad idea at the time of Christmas excesses. Therefore we have created a chapter of alternative feasting with some vegetarian offerings, some vegan dishes, and some dishes to make sure that the wheat allergy sufferer does not go without. We have also thrown in plenty of Christmas cheer with a chapter on party drinks for adults and kids alike, featuring both traditional Christmas flavors and colorfully themed drinks to help you celebrate the season.

Dust off the Bing Crosby and Elvis Presley CDs and get the season underway! If you are planning a Christmas party at home or have promised to bring some snacks to a party, take a look through our finger food chapter – there are some tasty treats perfect for a long night of partying, some hearty snacks to see you through the night one bite at a time, and also some more elegant offerings for that Christmas cocktail party. The big banquet chapter features large cuts and poultry for roasting, what many of us consider traditional Christmas fare. All this is complemented by a chapter of sauces, vegetables and side dishes to help create a truly stunning banquet for the big day.

In fact, this book has been designed so that if you make one recipe from each chapter you are guaranteed to create a special and memorable Christmas sure to please everybody.

A Movable Feast

The character of Christmas feasting has been changing as long as Christmas itself has been celebrated, since around the 4th century.

As Christianity eventually spread around the world, so Christmas as a celebration at the table evolved to take in the climates and characters of new communities, as it indeed continues to evolve and change today, even being celebrated as a cultural holiday by many non-Christians.

Regardless of your religious convictions, it is certain that the tradition of Christmas as a celebration will be with us as long as children gather excitedly under a tree, eager to open presents, and families make the effort to congregate, often from far flung locations around the globe.

Let's look beyond the scriptures at the history of Christmas banqueting and how it has evolved into its current form of celebration enjoyed today. Two thousand years ago, the middle of winter saw people in much of Europe with more time on their hands than other months – there was little to do in the fields, and animals were often kept under shelter. Naturally enough, people often turned to activities centerd around the hearth – feasting on large animals (which kept well once slaughtered in the coldest of weather), sitting around the fire relaxing with friends and family, perhaps having a drink of warmed wine. So winter festivals became very popular, as people were able to enjoy them a lot more than summer festivals, when there was much work to do every day, holiday or not. Many Christian practices usurped or borrowed from these earlier traditions as Christianity evolved, grew and assimilated local cultural practices.

Many traditions of the European winter solstice are the forerunners of the modern Christmas celebration, as the Fathers of the Church realised it would be easier to convert people to their new religion if they could associate the new festivals with their existing rites. Practices that were already entrenched were reformulated or moved in time (even if only by a few days) to accommodate the growing faith and celebration of Christianity. Practices that were perhaps less organised or formalized developed powerful meaning in the hands of the Church and became important elements in the story of the birth of Jesus and its related celebrations.

Many peoples celebrate Christmas with foods that are produced locally and only for Christmas. From the French 'Buche de Noel' (Christmas log) to egg-nog, spiced wine and minced pies, there are many examples of traditional fare that are familiar to us today or quite similar to something we ate or drank as a child.

Egg-nog is thought to have evolved out of the 17th century syllabub, when mulled or spiced wine heralded a time of great shipping advances and the spice trade.

The minced pie has its roots in medieval times, where minced anything was baked into a pie called a chewette, using fruits, meats, fish or whatever was at hand.

It became associated with the Christmas table around the 16th century, but it wasn't until the mid-19th century, when the meat started to disappear from the recipe (leaving only its fat or suet behind), that it began to resemble the fruit mince pie we recognise today.

The 12th night or king's cake is related to the stollen and other yeast cakes of medieval times, but this type of cake has proven popular on many different continents and is even associated in the Americas with the time of Mardi Gras, in the form of the king's cake. The tradition associated with king's cake harks back to finding the prize (a bean or small stone baked into the cake), the finder being crowned king of the harvest for the day. The 12th night cake is associated with the tradition of the Three Wise Men from the east, said to have visited the baby Jesus on the 12th night after his birth.

It is a basic French brioche dough filled with dried fruits and nuts, not dissimilar in many ways to the Italian panettone.

Ever since banqueting began to be incorporated into worship and share its symbolism, communities have organised themselves around food and the toil created to bring those foods to the table, celebrating the shared experience of work, weather and successful harvest. What better way to display and celebrate abundance than through good food, good company and good cheer?

Recent Traditions

In more modern times, Santa Claus has emerged as the chubby, merry gentleman in a bright red suit that children adore. The color of the suit comes from the colors of magazine illustrations from the 1860s, which in turn evolved from older traditions of Saint Nicholas and his various incarnations in different cultures.

By the early part of the 20th century he had been not only plumped up but also given a sack full of gifts with a workshop full of tinkering elves. Modern concepts of marketing have, for better or worse, seen the legend of Santa become one of the most recognisable symbols of Christmas, complete with a wife and a comfortable home somewhere in the Far North.

As well as the jolly man with gifts and more traditional rituals such as carolling and midnight mass, there are also traditional Christmas eating practices, for example, the Russian tradition of feasting that reminds us of the twelve Apostles by providing twelve courses for the banquet.

Even for the less religious among us, many Christian symbols usually adorn our Christmas tree or decorate the Christmas table, from the star of Bethlehem to the angels of heaven. For many, the meanings may have become somewhat obscured but the symbolism remains.

In today's busy world, older Christmas traditions such as nativity scenes are becoming less of a focus, being replaced by hectic December schedules and shopping sprees.

In many ways it can be comforting to recall that our Christmas feasts have their roots in the truly ancient practices that evolved in those long Northern winters. These Christmas banquets give everyone who sits down at the table a sense of fulfilment and belonging rarely achieved at any other time of year.

It is a time to be thankful for the company that you are in, the friends and family that you have to celebrate with, and the collective sense of peace and goodwill that we all share on a few very special days in the year.

Merry Christmas

to you and your loved ones, and have a joyous and happy new year.

Christmas Quiz

As a special treat we have prepared a quiz for you to do as a part of your Christmas day celebrations.

We have divided the questions into 3 sections – the last section is a little harder, while the first two sections are a little more child-friendly. You may want to make a game of it and photocopy the quiz pages for all who want to test their Christmas knowledge.

Alternatively, supply everybody with a pen and paper, have one person read the questions aloud to the group, then ask everybody to swap their answers and mark somebody else's. Also make sure that everybody puts their name at the top of their answers, to save any confusion when swapping around.

The answers and scores are on the pages following the quiz – no peeking! – and there is also a total score rating at the end. Good luck and have fun!

Multiple Choice

1. Who wrote the song *White Christmas*?
   A David Bowie
   B Bing Crosby
   C Irving Berlin
   D Sigue Sigue Sputnik

2. Of what country is St. Nicholas a patron saint?
   A The Czech Republic
   B Poland
   C New Zealand
   D Russia

3. Traditionally, what are German children not allowed to see until Christmas Eve?
   A Christmas sweets
   B Christmas stockings
   C The Christmas tree
   D Anybody wearing the colors green or red

4. What comes after '8 maids a-milking' in the song *The 12 days of Christmas*?
   A 9 singers singing
   B 9 lords a-leaping
   C 9 ladies dancing
   D 9 drummers drumming

5. What were the last words that Frosty the Snowman said?
   A I'll be back again someday
   B It's time to run away
   C My pipe is made of clay
   D I think I hear my mum calling

6. What is the name of the island in the Indian Ocean near Djakarta?
   A Yule Tidal Reef
   B Rudolf Island
   C Christmas Island
   D Boxing Day Island

7. Electric Christmas tree lights were first used in what year?
   A 1895
   B 1910
   C 1925
   D 1935

8. Good King Wenceslas was king of which country?
   A Hungary
   B Bohemia
   C Holland
   D Bolivia

9. In Sweden, the 'tomte' is a ...
   A Christmas cake
   B Christmas gnome
   C Special dance
   D Hat made of pine cones

10. How did 'Xmas' become an abbreviation for Christmas?
   A It is the American spelling for Christmas
   B It started as a spelling mistake
   C From the Greek word for Christ
   D From the Italian word for Christmas

11. Where would Rudolph 'go down'?
   A To the city
   B In history
   C By the river
   D Down, down, deeper down

12. What brought Frosty the Snowman to life?
   A Magic lotion
   B An old silk hat
   C A wish
   D A fairy

13. What did Frosty the Snowman carry down to the village?

A A broomstick in his hand
B A trumpet for the band
C A bucket full of sand
D A small plastic container with his sandwiches

14. What is the shape of the candy cane Christmas treat modelled after?

A The letter J for Jesus, turned upside down
B The Christmas zodiac symbol
C The walking cane Santa uses
D A shepherd's crook

15. How many lines of symmetry does a snowflake have?

A 6
B 8
C 10
D 12

16. What is a Kris Kringle?

A A lucky dip at Christmas time
B Swapping small gifts with friends or workmates
C Red or green potato chips available at Christmas
D A song used in an advertisement at Christmas time

17. Which of the following holidays DOES NOT take place in the month of December?

A Feast of St. Nicholas
B Candlemas
C Boxing Day
D Christmas Day

18. 'Hyvaa Joulua' is the Christmas greeting you will hear in which of these countries?

A Finland
B Poland
C Latvia
D Australia

19. Who sang White Christmas in the 1942 film Holiday Inn?

A Bob Hope
B Bing Crosby
C Frank Sinatra
D Frank Zappa

20. In which county will you be greeted 'God Jul'?

A Sweden
B Hawaii
C Hungary
D Uruguay

21. A special Christmas meal in France and Canada is called 'reveillon'. When is it eaten?

A After midnight mass
B During Sunday sermon
C On Boxing Day
D Any lunchtime in December

22. December 26th, also known as Boxing Day, is the holy day of which saint?

A St. Nicholas
B St. Stephen
C St. Francis
D St. Jerome

True or False

1. The goat is a Christmas symbol in Scandinavia.
   ❑ True ❑ False

2. In biblical times, shepherds were considered noble members of society.
   ❑ True ❑ False

3. 'Sretan Bozic' is the seasonal greeting you will hear in Bosnia.
   ❑ True ❑ False

4. Santa said 'Rudolph with your nose so bright, won't you ride my sleigh tonight'.
   ❑ True ❑ False

5. The tradition of kissing under the mistletoe started with a Scandinavian love goddess.
   ❑ True ❑ False

6. Royal Tannenbaum is the German botanist who discovered the Christmas tree.
   ❑ True ❑ False

7. The word 'carol' comes from the ancient Greek choros, which means 'dancing in a circle', and from the French word carole, meaning 'a song to accompany dancing'.
   ❑ True ❑ False

8. The Grinch not only stole Christmas, he stole Easter and lots of people's birthdays as well.
   ❑ True ❑ False

9. Tim Burton was the author of *The Nightmare before Christmas*.
   ❑ True ❑ False

10. Electric Christmas lights were invented in America by Thomas Edison.
   ❑ True ❑ False

11. All of the following films have Christmas as a part of their story: *Home Alone, Santa Claus conquers the Martians, Miracle on 34th street, Die hard*.
   ❑ True ❑ False

General Knowledge

1. What song was originally titled *One Horse Open Sleigh*?

2. What traditional European Christmas drink contains milk, sugar and eggs?

3. Name Santa's reindeer.

4. What is the character Scrooge's first name?

5. In the well-known cartoon *A Charlie Brown Christmas*, who is the director of the Christmas play?

6. What is the name of the last ghost in *A Christmas Carol*?

7. During the Christmas season traditional songs are sung. What is the name given to these types of songs?

8. What Christmas carol contains the word 'Fa-la-la-la-la-la-la-la-la'?

9. Which Christmas carol contains the line 'O tidings of comfort and joy'?

10. In *A Very Brady Christmas*, what happened to Mike Brady on Christmas Eve?

11. If you were caught standing under the mistletoe, what would you have to do?

12. What is the traditional Christmas decorative plant with small berries and red leaves?

13. 'Buon Natale' is the Christmas greeting in which country?

14. Which of these actors were born on Christmas Day?
A Humphrey Bogart, born 1899
B Sissy Spacek, born 1949
C Sarah Jessica Parker, born 1965

15. In which country will you hear the greeting 'Zalig Kerstfeest'?

16. 'Joyeux Noel' is a European Christmas greeting also heard in parts of Canada. What language is this phrase?

17. Which English-speaking country only declared Christmas Day a public holiday in 1958?

18. Which part of the community is saint St. Nicholas the saint of?
A Children
B Shepherds and cowhands
C Merchants and sailors
D Wealthy German industrialists

19. In the song *The 12 days of Christmas*, what gift was given to the true love on the second day?

20. What was the first gift my true love sent on the sixth day of Christmas?

21. Was St. Nick a cartoon character?

22. Who wrote the popular American Christmas story *The Grinch*?

Answers and Scores

(Top score for this section – 100 points)

QUESTION 1 (5 POINTS)
C Irving Berlin

QUESTION 2 (5 POINTS)
D Russia

QUESTION 3 (3 POINTS)
C The Christmas tree

QUESTION 4 (5 POINTS)
C 9 ladies dancing

QUESTION 5 (5 POINTS)
A 'I'll be back again someday'

QUESTION 6 (3 POINTS)
C Christmas Island

QUESTION 7 (5 POINTS)
A 1895

QUESTION 8 (5 POINTS)
B Bohemia

QUESTION 9 (5 POINTS)
B Christmas gnome

QUESTION 10 (5 POINTS)
C From the Greek word for Christ

QUESTION 11 (5 POINTS)
B In history

QUESTION 12 (5 POINTS)
B An old silk hat

QUESTION 13 (3 POINTS)
A A broomstick in his hand

QUESTION 14 (5 POINTS)
D A shepherd's crook

QUESTION 15 (5 POINTS)
A 6

QUESTION 16 (3 POINTS)
B Swapping small gifts with friends or workmates

QUESTION 17 (5 POINTS)
B Candlemas

QUESTION 18 (5 POINTS)
A Finland

QUESTION 19 (3 POINTS)
B Bing Crosby

QUESTION 20 (5 POINTS)
A Sweden

QUESTION 21 (5 POINTS)
A After midnight mass

QUESTION 22 (5 POINTS)
B St. Stephen

(Top score for this section – 49 points)

QUESTION 1 (5 POINTS)
True.

QUESTION 2 (5 POINTS)
False. They were considered very low class.

QUESTION 3 (5 POINTS)
True.

QUESTION 4 (3 POINTS)
False. Santa said 'Rudolph with your nose so bright, won't you drive my sleigh tonight'.

QUESTION 5 (5 POINTS)
True.

QUESTION 6 (3 POINTS)
False. Tannenbaum is the German name for the Christmas tree. Royal Tannenbaum is a movie character played by Gene Hackman.

QUESTION 7 (5 POINTS)
True.

QUESTION 8 (3 POINTS)
False.

QUESTION 9 (5 POINTS)
True.

QUESTION 10 (5 POINTS)
False. They were invented by Edward Hibberd Johnson, an associate of Edison's.

QUESTION 11 (5 POINTS)
True.

GENERAL KNOWLEDGE

(Top score for this section – 53 points)

QUESTION 1 (3 POINTS)
Jingle Bells

QUESTION 2 (3 POINTS)
Eggnog

QUESTION 3 (5 POINTS PER REINDEER)
Dasher, Dancer, Prancer, Vixen, Comet, Cupid, Donner (or Dunder), Blitzen (or Blixem). There were originally eight reindeer

Rudolph was a late addition because of the popularity song. (3 points for Rudolph)

QUESTION 4 (3 POINTS)
Ebenezer

QUESTION 5 (5 POINTS)
Lucy

QUESTION 6 (5 POINTS)
The Ghost of Christmas Yet to Come

QUESTION 7 (3 POINTS)
Carols

QUESTION 8 (3 POINTS)
Deck the Halls

QUESTION 9 (5 POINTS)
God Rest Ye Merry Gentlemen

QUESTION 10 (5 POINTS)
Mike Brady (the father) is trapped in a cave-in

QUESTION 11 (3 POINTS)
You would have to kiss someone

QUESTION 12 (3 POINTS)
Mistletoe

QUESTION 13 (5 POINTS)
Italy

QUESTION 14 (5 POINTS PER PERSON)
A Humphrey Bogart
B Sissy Spacek

QUESTION 15 (5 POINTS)
Belgium

QUESTION 16. (3 POINTS)
French

QUESTION 17 (5 POINTS)
Scotland

QUESTION 18 (5 POINTS PER ANSWER)
A Children
C Merchants and sailors

QUESTION 19 (3 POINTS)
Two turtle doves

QUESTION 20 (3 POINTS)
Six geese a-laying

QUESTION 21 (3 POINTS)
No, he was a Saint (Saint Nicholas) who looked out for the poor and gave them gifts

QUESTION 22 (3 POINTS)
Dr. Seuss

Score
Your Quiz…

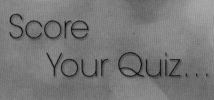

- ✪ **PERFECT SCORE 202**
  Excellent

- ✪ **BETWEEN 201–151**
  Very very good

- ✪ **BETWEEN 150–101**
  Very good

- ✪ **BETWEEN 100–51**
  Almost as good
  as very good

- ✪ **BETWEEN 50–0**
  Almost as good
  as almost very good

Christmas is party season, so we have
gathered an exciting selection of finger food
recipes to make your party extra-special.
Some sophisticated and robust snacks are
a great idea for helping everybody survive
all that free-flowing Christmas cheer! These
snacks are elegant and impressive but not too
complicated, so you can prepare them easily
and speedily, which will please both the chef
and the crowd.

Christmas
Party

COLLECTORS EDITION

Christmas Party

COLLECTORS EDITION

The Ritz's Egg Sandwiches

PREPARATION 1 hr 20 mins

5 hard-boiled eggs, shelled

dash of Tabasco sauce

10 slices white bread

1 oz/30g butter, at room temperature

¼ bunch watercress

MAYONNAISE

1 egg yolk

½ teaspoon salt

½ teaspoon wholegrain mustard

⅔ cup extra-light virgin olive oil

1 teaspoon sherry vinegar

freshly ground black pepper

1 To make the mayonnaise, place egg yolk, salt and mustard in a bowl. Beat vigorously with a wooden spoon until thickened. Add quarter of the oil drop by drop, then stir in half the vinegar.

2 Gradually add remaining oil in a thin stream, beating constantly. Stir in remaining vinegar and season to taste with black pepper. If too thin, add 1–2 tablespoons boiling hot water, beating well.

3 Roughly chop hard-boiled eggs and stir into mayonnaise. Season to taste with Tabasco. Butter the bread, then spread egg mixture on half the slices, top with watercress and remaining bread slices. Press firmly, wrap and chill for 1 hour. Trim crusts and cut each sandwich into fingers.

Lemon Chicken Fingers

Lemon Chicken Fingers

PREPARATION 40 mins   **COOKING** 25 mins

2 lb/1 kg chicken breast fillets

oil for deep frying

MARINADE

2 tablespoons soy sauce

¼ cup sherry

1 in/25mm piece fresh ginger, grated

zest of 1 lemon

2 teaspoons sugar

BATTER

2 egg whites

¼ cup all-purpose flour

¼ cup lemon juice

DIPPING SAUCE

½ cup chicken stock

2 tablespoons lemon juice

2 tablespoons cornstarch

1 Cut the chicken into ⅓ in/1cm-wide strips from the long side of the fillet. Place strips in a non-metallic dish. Combine marinade ingredients, pour over chicken strips, mix well and allow to marinate for 30 minutes.

2 To make the batter, beat the egg whites to soft peaks, fold in flour and lemon juice.

3 Heat oil in a deep fryer to 360°F/180°C. Remove the strips from marinade, reserving the marinade. Dip 5 strips at a time into the batter and deep-fry for 5 minutes until golden. Drain on absorbent paper. Repeat with remainder.

4 To make the dipping sauce, pour reserved marinade into a saucepan, add chicken stock and bring to the boil. Mix the lemon juice and cornstarch to a smooth paste, stir into the saucepan, lower heat and stir until sauce boils and thickens. Drizzle sauce over chicken fingers and serve.

Olive Rounds with Goat's Cheese

makes 60

Olive Rounds with Goat's Cheese

PREPARATION 2hrs 20 mins   **COOKING** 12 mins

2 cups all-purpose flour

2 teaspoons baking powder

¼ teaspoon salt

⅛ teaspoon sugar

5 oz/150g butter, chilled and diced

2½ oz/75g Parmesan cheese, grated

½ cup milk

3½ oz/100g pitted black olives, finely chopped

TOPPING

½ cup heavy cream

8 oz/225g goat's cheese

1 roasted red pepper, cut into thin strips

½ small bunch fresh chervil

1 Combine the flour, baking powder, salt, sugar and butter in a food processor. Add the Parmesan and ⅓ cup of the milk and process into a smooth dough. Add the olives and the remaining milk.

2 Flour your hands and shape the dough into a ball, then divide in half and place each half on a sheet of plastic wrap. Roll each dough into a neat cylinder shape 2 in/5cm in diameter, wrap around the plastic wrap and twist the ends to firm up the shape (finished dough will look like a Christmas bon bon). Refrigerate for 2 hours.

3 Preheat oven to 360°F/180°C and line 2 oven trays with baking paper. Unwrap the chilled dough and cut into ¼ in/5mm-thick slices with a sharp knife. Place the slices 2 in/5cm apart on the trays and bake for 10–12 minutes until the edges are firm and golden and the bottoms are lightly browned. Cool on a rack.

4 Meanwhile, prepare the topping. Work the cream into the goat's cheese to make a smooth paste.

5 When the olive rounds have cooled, top each with 1 teaspoon of cheese mixture and a piece of red pepper, then finish with a sprig of chervil.

Cheese Tartlets

makes 20

Cheese Tartlets

PREPARATION 35 mins   COOKING 20 mins

8 oz/250g all-purpose flour

½ teaspoon salt

4 oz/125g butter, chilled
and diced

1 oz/30g black olives,
chopped

1 cup heavy cream

3½ oz/100g aged Cheddar
cheese, grated

1 egg, beaten

2 oz/60g Stilton or other blue
cheese, crumbled

1 Sift flour and salt into a bowl. Rub in butter until mixture resembles coarse breadcrumbs. Gradually add 3 tablespoons iced water, mixing to make a smooth dough. Shape into a ball, wrap in plastic wrap and chill for 30 minutes.

2 Preheat oven to 360°F/180°C. Roll out pastry and cut out 20 rounds using a 3 in/75mm cutter. Place rounds in tartlet molds and chill for 15 minutes, then prick the bottoms of each pastry with a fork. Bake for 10 minutes.

3 Meanwhile combine olives, cream, Cheddar, egg and Stilton and mix well. Spoon mixture into the tartlet cases.

4 Bake tartlets for a further 10 minutes or until golden. Serve warm.

Onion Cumin Tartlets

makes 16

Onion Cumin Tartlets

PREPARATION 45 mins   COOKING 30 mins

2 sheets ready-rolled
puff pastry

1½ oz/45g butter

1 teaspoon cumin seeds

1 small onion, finely sliced

1 egg

½ cup heavy cream

freshly ground black pepper

1 Cut pastry into 3 in/75mm circles. Push the pastry down firmly into fluted tartlet molds and chill for 30 minutes.

2 Preheat oven to 430°F/220°C. Bake pastry for 5 minutes or until just firm, reduce the heat to 400°F/200°C and cook for 5 minutes longer or until just golden. Cool.

3 Meanwhile, melt the butter in a skillet over moderate heat until hot and foaming, add cumin seeds and onion and cook, stirring, until onion is soft and transparent. Drain well. In a separate bowl, whisk together egg, cream and black pepper.

4 Reduce oven temperature to 360°F/180°C. Push the bottom of the pastry cases down if they have puffed up and spread onion mixture evenly into the bottom of each case. Pour in egg mixture and bake for 15 minutes or until golden. Serve warm.

makes 60

Rosemary Cookies with Anchovy and Parmesan

PREPARATION 2 hrs 20 mins   COOKING 10 mins

4 oz/125g butter

13 oz/375g cream cheese, at room temperature

⅔ cup all-purpose flour, sifted

1 sprig rosemary, leaves removed and finely chopped

pinch of Cayenne pepper

8 anchovies

3½ oz/100g Parmesan cheese, grated

zest of 3 lemons

juice of half a lemon

1 Beat together butter and ⅓ of the cream cheese until well blended. Add flour, rosemary and Cayenne and mix with a fork until combined.

2 Place dough onto 2 large sheets of plastic wrap. Roll each dough into a neat cylinder shape 1½ in/4cm in diameter, wrap around the plastic wrap and twist the ends to firm up the shape (finished dough will look like a Christmas bon bon). Refrigerate for 2 hours.

3 Preheat oven to 400°F/200°C and lightly butter 3 baking sheets. Cut rolls into ¼ in/5mm-thick slices, place on baking sheets and bake for 8–10 minutes or until golden.

4 Meanwhile, put anchovies, Parmesan, ⅓ of the lemon zest, the lemon juice and the remaining cream cheese into a food processor. Blend for a short amount of time until a medium-to-rough paste forms. Top each cookie with a teaspoon of the anchovy paste and sprinkle with a little of the remaining lemon zest.

Note Pastry can be frozen for up to 6 months.

makes 15

Christmas Scones with Roe Aïoli

PREPARATION 15 mins   COOKING 15 mins

2 cups all-purpose flour

2 teaspoons baking powder

2 teaspoons sugar

1 oz/30g butter, cubed

⅔ cup buttermilk

3½ oz/100g cooked shrimp, peeled, deveined and coarsely chopped

¼ cup mayonnaise

¼ cup sour cream

3–4 sprigs fresh dill, chopped

salt and freshly ground black pepper

2 oz/60g salmon or trout roe

1 Preheat oven to 440°F/220°C and line an oven tray with baking paper. Combine flour, baking powder and sugar in a bowl. Add butter and lightly rub into flour using fingertips. Make a well in the center of the flour. Pour in buttermilk and, using a knife, mix to a soft, sticky dough. Turn onto a floured board and knead lightly. Roll out dough to 1 in/25mm thick on an oven tray and cut out star shapes, then separate the shapes so they have room to expand when cooking. Bake for 10–15 minutes or until golden.

2 Mix the shrimp, mayonnaise, sour cream and dill. Season with salt and pepper, then fold through the roe. Remove scones from the oven and allow to cool on the tray.

3 Split the large stars open and fill with the aïoli. For the smaller in-between shapes, top with a teaspoon of mixture and garnish with an extra sprig of dill. Fit the shapes together again like a jigsaw to serve.

Potato Omelet

serves 8

Potato Omelet

PREPARATION 4 mins   COOKING 12 mins

2 lb/1 kg potatoes, peeled

1 cup olive oil

1 small onion, finely diced

salt and freshly ground black pepper

5 eggs, beaten

1 Wash and dry potatoes, then cut into thin slices. Heat the oil in a skillet, add potatoes and onion, season and cover. Fry gently, moving the skillet so the vegetables don't stick, and take care the potatoes don't become crisp.

2 Once potatoes are cooked, break them up a little and remove from the skillet with a slotted spoon. Add to the beaten eggs and stir until they are well covered. Add a little more salt, if desired.

3 Remove most of the oil from the skillet, leaving about 1 tablespoon, and reheat. Have ready a plate with a slightly larger diameter than the skillet. Return egg and potato mixture to the skillet and cook for a few minutes until one side is golden. Carefully slip the omelet onto the plate, cooked-side down, and then slip it back into the skillet, cooked-side up. Cook until firm. Cut into bite-size wedges to serve.

Liver and Sage Toasts

makes 40

Liver and Sage Toasts

PREPARATION 15 mins   COOKING 8 mins

1 oz/30g unsalted butter

½ onion, chopped

1 tablespoon capers, chopped

6 fresh sage leaves

1 tablespoon dry sherry

freshly ground black pepper

½ small bunch fresh parsley, chopped

1 tablespoon olive oil

1 lb/500g chicken livers, trimmed and chopped

4 oz/125g Parmesan cheese, grated

juice of 1 lemon

3 oz/90g pack of mini toasts

1 Melt butter in a skillet over moderately low heat and cook onion until soft. Add capers, sage, sherry and black pepper and simmer, stirring, until most of the liquid evaporates. Cool slightly, add the parsley and transfer to a food processor.

2 In a clean skillet, heat oil over moderately high heat and sauté livers for 1–2 minutes or until brown on the outside but still pink inside. Add to onion mixture and process to make a coarse purée. Fold in the Parmesan and lemon juice.

3 Top each toast with a teaspoon of topping and serve.

makes 24

Baby Brioche Bites

PREPARATION 12 hrs   COOKING 18 mins

DOUGH

1 teaspoon dried yeast

8 oz/250g all-purpose flour

1½ tablespoons superfine
sugar

½ teaspoon salt

3 eggs, plus 1 egg yolk

5 oz/150g unsalted butter,
melted and cooled

FILLING

juice of 1 lemon

1 lb/500g cream cheese,
at room temperature

½ small bunch fresh dill,
finely chopped

½ small bunch fresh chives,
finely chopped

½ medium red onion, grated

4 oz/125g smoked salmon
slices, cut into 3–4 pieces each

1 To make dough, mix yeast to a paste with
2 tablespoons warm water. Fit food processor
with a plastic blade, add flour, sugar and salt
and process briefly to combine.

2 Add eggs, butter and yeast mixture to flour
and process until just combined. Transfer to a
buttered bowl, press a piece of plastic wrap
onto surface of dough and cover bowl tightly
with more wrap. Refrigerate overnight.

3 Using the smallest fluted tartlet molds
available, break off small pieces of dough, roll
into balls and place in molds, filling them no
more than two-thirds. Place molds on a baking
sheet, cover with a towel and set aside in a
warm place until dough has risen to almost fill
the molds.

4 Preheat oven to 400°F/200°C. Mix the egg
yolk with 1 teaspoon water and a pinch of salt,
brush tops of brioches with egg mixture and
bake for 15–18 minutes or until golden. Stand
5 minutes in molds before turning out to cool.

5 To make the filling, add lemon juice to the
cream cheese and beat until smooth, then
stir in herbs and onion. Slice halfway through
the tops of each brioche on an angle, liberally
spread with cream cheese mixture, and add a
curl of salmon. Cover and store in a cool place
for no longer than 3 hours before serving.

makes 36 | # Vegetable Triangles

PREPARATION 15 mins   COOKING 25 mins

1 bunch spinach, finely chopped

1 large onion, chopped

3 medium sebago potatoes, peeled and diced

5 oz/140g pumpkin, diced

1 carrot, peeled and diced

½ oz/15g butter

salt and freshly ground black pepper

small bunch freshly parsley, chopped

4 sheets ready-rolled puff pastry

½ cup milk

1 Combine the spinach, onion, potatoes, pumpkin and carrot and steam for 8–10 minutes. Drain well, then mash. Add butter, salt, pepper and parsley.

2 Preheat oven to 400°F/200°C and line 3 oven trays with baking paper. Cut each sheet of pastry into 9 equal squares. Place a heaped teaspoon of vegetable mixture on one corner of each pastry square. Brush edges with milk, then fold pastry over to form a triangle. Press edges together to seal well. Brush with a little milk and bake for 10–15 minutes.

If you have chosen to have your Christmas this year in a warmer climate, as many people now do, we have prepared a more contemporary group of recipes to accent that luxurious poolside feel. If you find yourself in the middle of a white Christmas you can turn up the heater and have a winter tropical party with these recipes. Or if you are actually on location, roll up the cane shutters, order a morning cocktail and prepare your fish market shopping list!

Elegant Casual

COLLECTORS EDITION

Elegant Casual

COLLECTORS EDITION

Broiled Oysters with Champagne and Cream

serves 4

PREPARATION 2 mins   COOKING 7 mins

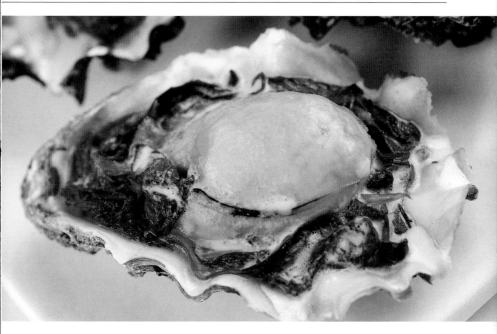

12 fresh oysters in their shells, pre-shucked

½ cup fish stock

¼ cup Champagne

1 oz/30g butter

2 tablespoons heavy cream

freshly ground black pepper

2 oz/60g baby spinach

1 Place the oyster shells in a flameproof dish lined with crumpled foil so that the shells sit level.

2 Bring the fish stock to a simmer and poach the oysters for 30–60 seconds, until just firm. Remove from the pan, add the Champagne and boil for 2 minutes to reduce. Remove from the heat and whisk in the butter, then the cream. Season with pepper.

3 Preheat the broiler to high. Cook the spinach in a saucepan of water for 2–3 minutes until wilted. Squeeze out the excess liquid and divide between the shells. Top with an oyster and spoon over a little sauce. Cook close to the broiler for 1 minute or until heated through.

Barbecued Seafood Salad

PREPARATION 1 hr 15 mins   **COOKING** 8 mins

2 tablespoons lemon juice

1 tablespoon olive oil

10 oz/300g firm white fish such as swordfish, mackerel or cod, cut into 1 in/25mm cubes

10 oz/300g pink fish such as salmon, marlin or tuna, cut into 1 in/25mm cubes

12 scallops

12 uncooked shrimp (with or without shell)

1 calamari tube, cut into rings

1 bunch watercress, broken into sprigs

1 large red onion, cut into rings

1 long cucumber, peeled and thinly sliced

RASPBERRY AND TARRAGON DRESSING

3 sprigs tarragon, leaves removed and stalks discarded

2 tablespoons raspberry or red wine vinegar

2 tablespoons lemon juice

1 tablespoon olive oil

freshly ground black pepper

1 Place lemon juice and oil in a bowl. Whisk to combine. Add white and pink fish, scallops, shrimp and calamari. Toss to combine. Cover and marinate in the refrigerator for 1 hour or until ready to use (do not marinate for longer than 2 hours).

2 For the dressing, place tarragon, vinegar, lemon juice, oil and black pepper in a screw-top jar. Shake to combine and set aside.

3 Preheat a barbecue or broiler until very hot. Line a serving platter with watercress. Drain seafood mixture and place on barbecue plate or in pan. Add onion and cook, turning several times, for 6–8 minutes or until seafood is just cooked. Take care not to overcook or the seafood will be tough and dry.

4 Transfer seafood to a bowl. Add cucumber and dressing. Toss to combine. Spoon seafood mixture over watercress and serve immediately.

serves 4

Baby Octopus Salad

PREPARATION 1 hr 15 mins   **COOKING** 8 mins

2 lb/1 kg baby octopus, cleaned and trimmed

1 in/25mm piece fresh ginger, grated

juice of 1 lime

½ cup peanut oil

1 teaspoon sesame oil

2 tablespoons kecap manis

3 cloves garlic, crushed

1 Place octopus in a glass bowl. Combine the remaining ingredients and pour over the octopus. Cover and refrigerate for 1 hour or longer, overnight if preferred.

2 Preheat the hotplate of a barbecue. Drain the octopus and reserve the marinade. Cook octopus until the tentacles are very curly and dark in color. Turn octopus frequently and add a little extra marinade during cooking.

3 Serve the octopus tossed through a large mixed-leaf salad.

Chermoula Shrimp

makes 8

Chermoula Shrimp

PREPARATION 4 hrs   **COOKING** 3 mins

24 green shrimp, heads and
shells removed

¼ small red onion, roughly
chopped

2 cloves garlic, roughly
chopped

⅓ cup cilantro

⅓ cup mint

⅓ cup flat-leaf parsley

1 small red chili, deseeded
and chopped

1 teaspoon ground cumin

½ teaspoon sweet paprika

2 tablespoons lime juice

2 tablespoons olive oil

2 limes, cut into wedges

1 Soak 8 bamboo skewers in water for
30 minutes. Remove veins from shrimp.
Thread 3 shrimp onto each skewer and
place in a shallow dish.

2 Place onion, garlic, cilantro, mint, parsley,
chili, cumin, paprika, lime juice and olive oil in
a food processor. Process until smooth. Coat
shrimp in marinade, cover with plastic wrap
and refrigerate for 3–4 hours.

3 Cook shrimp on a barbecue grill or
char-grill for 2–3 minutes or until cooked.
Serve with lime wedges.

Butterflied Shrimp with Garlic, Chili and Parsley

serves 6

Butterflied Shrimp with Garlic, Chili and Parsley

PREPARATION 3 hrs   COOKING 15 mins

2 lb/1 kg green shrimp, shelled but with tails intact

2 tablespoons olive oil

1 tablespoon lemon juice

2 cloves garlic, crushed

2 red chilies, deseeded and finely chopped

¼ cup parsley, chopped

oil for deep-frying

½ cup all-purpose flour

2 lemons, cut into wedges

1 Cut shrimp down the back and remove vein. Combine oil, lemon juice, garlic, chili and parsley in a bowl. Add shrimp, mix well, and leave to marinate for 2–3 hours.

2 Heat oil in a large pan. Coat shrimp with flour, drop in oil in batches and cook quickly in oil for 2–3 minutes. Drain on absorbent paper. Serve with lemon wedges and extra parsley.

Broiled Shellfish with Chili Salsa

Broiled Shellfish with Chili Salsa

PREPARATION 10 mins **COOKING** 15 mins

2 cooked lobsters or crayfish,
about 23 oz/650g each

1 tablespoon peanut oil

½ teaspon Cayenne pepper

¼ cup cilantro

SALSA

⅓ cup extra-virgin olive oil

1 red pepper, deseeded
and diced

½ small onion, finely chopped

1 small red chili, deseeded
and finely chopped

½ teaspoon smoked paprika

1 tablespoon sun-dried
tomato paste

zest and juice of 1 lime,
plus 1 whole lime

salt and freshly ground
black pepper

1 To make the salsa, heat the oil in a saucepan and fry the red pepper, onion, chili and paprika for 5 minutes. Stir in the tomato paste, lime zest and lime juice and season to taste. Transfer to a bowl. Peel and segment the whole lime, cut into small pieces and set aside.

2 To cut the lobsters in half lengthwise, turn one on its back. Using a large sharp knife, cut through the head end first, then turn the lobster around and cut through the tail end. Discard the small greyish sac in the head and the black thread running down the back. Crack the large claws with a small hammer or wooden rolling pin. Repeat with the second lobster.

3 Heat a large non-stick skillet or heavy ridged cast-iron grill pan until very hot. Add the peanut oil and Cayenne, quickly add the lobster halves cut-side down and cook for 2–3 minutes. Scatter the lobster with salsa, lime segments and cilantro. Serve immediately with the extra salsa at the side.

Shellfish with Brandy Tarragon Butter

Shellfish with Brandy Tarragon Butter

PREPARATION 10 mins   COOKING 12 mins

2 lobsters or crayfish,
about 23 oz/650g each

salt and freshly ground
black pepper

2 oz/60g butter, melted

1 tablespoon olive oil

4 tablespoons brandy

4 sprigs tarragon, leaves
removed and stalks discarded

1 Rinse the lobsters under cold running water and dry with absorbent paper. To cut the lobsters in half lengthwise, turn one on its back. Using a large sharp knife, cut through the head end first, then turn the lobster around and cut through the tail end. Discard the small greyish sac in the head and the black thread running down the back. Season with salt and pepper and generously brush all over the cut surface with half the melted butter.

2 Preheat oven to 400°F/200°C. Add the oil to a large ovenproof skillet and sauté lobster for 2–3 minutes, then place in the oven for a further 8 minutes.

3 Transfer lobster from the skillet onto a platter. Add the brandy, remaining butter and the tarragon to the skillet and cook over a high heat for 30–60 seconds until it starts to foam and the butter browns slightly. Pour sauce over lobster and serve.

serves 4

Lobster Mornay

PREPARATION 15 mins   COOKING 8 mins

2 medium lobsters, cooked
and halved

MORNAY SAUCE

1¼ cups milk

1 bay leaf

1 small onion, chopped

5 black peppercorns

1 oz/30g butter, plus ½ oz/15g

2 tablespoons all-purpose flour

¼ cup heavy cream

2 oz/60g Cheddar cheese,
grated

salt and freshly ground
black pepper

2 oz/60g fresh breadcrumbs

1 Remove the lobster meat from the shells and cut into bite-size pieces. Reserve the shells.

2 In a saucepan, place the milk, bay leaf, onion and peppercorns. Heat slowly to boiling point. Remove from the heat, cover and stand for 10 minutes. Strain.

3 In a pan, melt 1 oz/30g butter, then remove from the heat. Stir in the flour and blend, gradually adding the strained milk. Return the pan to the heat, and stir constantly until the sauce boils and thickens. Simmer for 1 minute, remove from the heat, add the cream, cheese, salt and pepper. Stir the sauce until the cheese melts, then add the lobster.

4 Divide the mixture between the shells. Melt the remaining butter in a small pan, add the breadcrumbs, and stir to combine. Scatter the crumbs over the lobster and brown under a hot broiler.

Crayfish with Green Herbs

PREPARATION 20 mins   **COOKING** 30 mins

23 oz/650g crayfish or lobster

3 tablespoons extra-virgin
olive oil

salt and freshly ground
black pepper

2 small potatoes, peeled

2 medium tomatoes, diced

¼ avocado, diced

1 small Lebanese cucumber,
peeled and diced

1 sprig chervil, chopped

1 sprig tarragon, leaves
removed and stalk discarded

1 oz/30g baby Romaine lettuce

BOUQUET GARNI

3 sprigs parsley

2 large bay leaves

3 sprigs thyme

3 sprigs tarragon

COURT BOUILLON

2 cups dry white wine

2 carrots, peeled and sliced

2 stalks celery, sliced

1 onion, sliced

1½ teaspoons coarse sea salt

5 black peppercorns

1 Prepare the bouquet garni. Bundle the herbs together and tie firmly with kitchen string.

2 To make the court bouillon, combine the white wine, vegetables, sea salt, peppercorns, the bouquet garni and 4 cups water. Bring to the boil, then immerse the lobster for 6 minutes. Drain and allow to cool.

3 Remove the meat from the shell, keeping the tail intact. Extract all the meat from the joints and legs. Slice the lobster tail into medallions and finely dice the meat from the legs along with the small end pieces of the tail. Drizzle the lobster tail medallions with 1 tablespoon oil, season with salt and freshly ground black pepper, then lightly broil.

4 Cook the potatoes in boiling water until cooked, about 20 minutes. While still warm, slice the potatoes into small rounds and set aside. Combine the tomato, avocado and cucumber with the herbs and the chopped lobster, and season to taste.

5 Divide the tomato mixture between 4 serving plates. Place the lettuce on top, then finish with the broiled lobster medallions and potato slices. Drizzle with the remaining olive oil and serve.

Shellfish and Smoked Trout Salad

Shellfish and Smoked Trout Salad

PREPARATION 15 mins

1 cooked lobster or crayfish

14 oz/400g smoked trout

1 Continental cucumber

1 carrot, peeled

1 green courgette

1 yellow courgette

3½ oz/100g tatsoi leaves

DRESSING

juice of 2 limes

1 tablespoon palm sugar

½ cup olive oil

salt and freshly ground black pepper

1 Remove the meat from the tail of the lobster, slice finely and set aside. Alternatively, ask your fishmonger to do this for you. Cut the smoked trout into thin strips and set aside.

2 Slice the cucumber in half lengthwise, then scoop out and discard the seeds. Slice on a mandoline or use a vegetable peeler to make long, skinny strips resembling fettuccine. Slice the carrot in the same manner. Keeping the courgette whole, slice lengthwise into long thin strips.

3 Gently mix the lobster, trout, cut vegetables and tatsoi leaves.

4 For the dressing, heat the lime juice and palm sugar until the sugar dissolves. Pour into a bowl and whisk in the olive oil until the mixture is thick and the oil has emulsified with the lime juice. Season with salt and pepper and mix this through the salad ingredients. Arrange the salad on an attractive platter and serve.

Salmon with Onion and Red Wine Butter

serves 4

PREPARATION 1 hr 10 mins   **COOKING** 15 mins

½ cup red wine

½ small red onion, finely chopped

2½ oz/75g butter, at room temperature

¼ cup fresh parsley, finely chopped

1 clove garlic, very finely chopped

sea salt and freshly ground black pepper

1 tablespoon sunflower oil

4 salmon fillets, about 6 oz/175g each, skinned

1 Place the wine and onion in a small saucepan and bring to the boil. Boil rapidly for about 4–5 minutes over a high heat or until reduced to about 2 tablespoons. Remove from the heat and allow to cool completely.

2 In a bowl, beat the butter until smooth, add the parsley, garlic, seasoning and reduced wine and mix together with a fork. Place the butter in plastic wrap on a piece of baking paper and roll up into a tight sausage shape. Refrigerate until hardened.

3 Heat the oil in a large skillet over a medium heat and cook the salmon for 4 minutes. Turn and cook for 3–4 minutes more, until cooked through. Cut the butter into four pieces, place one on top of each salmon fillet, and cook for 2 minutes more before serving.

For many of us, this is what Christmas is all about
– a roast turkey or goose, roast beef or a ham
(or, if we're lucky enough, one of each!).
Christmas is a great opportunity to cook those
special meals we remember so fondly from our
childhood, those meals that were so delicious
we just couldn't resist going back for seconds,
or even thirds. These recipes are the reason our
willpower breaks down at Christmas and we have
to have another helping – they are just so good.

The Big Banquet

COLLECTORS EDITION

The Big Banquet

COLLECTORS EDITION

serves 6 | Roast Pork

PREPARATION 15 mins **COOKING** 1 hr 45 mins

3 lb/1½ kg boned loin of pork

2 tablespoons olive oil

salt

APRICOT AND MACADAMIA STUFFING

½ cup dried apricots, finely chopped

¼ cup macadamias, chopped

3 green onions, sliced

zest of 1 orange

1 teaspoon mixed herbs

¼ cup sage, chopped

¾ cup fresh breadcrumbs

1 oz/30g butter, melted

1 Combine all stuffing ingredients in a bowl and set aside. Preheat the oven to 440°F/220°C.

2 Score the pork rind with a sharp knife. Lay the pork fat-side down on a clean surface. Cut a slit into the pork, being careful not to cut all the way through. Spread the stuffing evenly over the pork and roll up. Tie with string at regular intervals. Place pork on a rack over a baking tray. Brush with olive oil and massage the salt into the skin.

3 Bake for 20–30 minutes, reduce the heat to 360°F/180°C and continue to cook for 1–1½ hours or until cooked when tested with a skewer. Remove from the oven and cover with foil. Leave to stand for 15 minutes before slicing. Serve with roast potatoes and pumpkin.

serves 20–30

Stout-Glazed Ham

PREPARATION 40 mins   COOKING 3 hrs 35 mins

16 lb/7½ kg cooked leg
of ham

40 cloves

2 cups stout beer

6 oz/170g soft brown sugar

2 tablespoons mustard

1 teaspoon ground ginger

2 teaspoons ground
cardamom

1 Preheat oven to 320°F/160°C. Remove the skin from the ham leaving a portion of skin around the bone. Score the ham with diagonal lines in both directions and put a clove in the center of each section. Place ham fat-side up in a roasting dish and pour over 1¾ cups of the stout. Bake for 3 hours, basting occasionally with stout. Remove ham from oven and baste thoroughly.

2 Increase oven temperature to 400°F/200°C. Combine sugar, mustard, ginger, cardamom and enough remaining stout to make a paste. Spread mixture over ham and bake for 35 minutes or until well glazed.

Quail with Grapes

PREPARATION 10 mins   COOKING 10 mins

6 quail, butterflied

salt and freshly ground

black pepper

3 oz/90g butter

1 cup dry red wine

2 teaspoons sugar

2 tablespoons lemon juice

3½ oz/100g red seedless

grapes, halved

1 Preheat oven to 400°F/200°C. Pat birds dry and season with salt and black pepper to taste. Melt butter in a shallow flameproof casserole or large skillet over a moderate heat and cook quail until golden on all sides. Cook in preheated oven for 5 minutes.

2 Meanwhile, pour wine, sugar and lemon juice into a small saucepan and bring to the boil. Reduce heat to low and simmer gently for 10 minutes. Add grapes and cook for 5 minutes longer. Serve sauce over quail.

Note Ask your butcher to butterfly your quail for you.

serves 6

Glazed Poussin

PREPARATION 30 mins   COOKING 1 hr 15 mins

6 x 1 lb/500g poussin

1 oz/30g butter

5 oz/150g watercress

PINE NUT STUFFING

2 oz/60g unsalted butter

3 scallions, finely chopped

6 oz/180g stale bread, diced

1 stalk celery, finely chopped

3 oz/90g golden raisins

1 oz/30g pine nuts, chopped

¼ bunch flat-leaf parsley, finely chopped

zest of ½ orange

zest of ½ lemon

salt and freshly ground black pepper

½ cup dry white wine or orange juice

MANGO CHUTNEY GLAZE

2 oz/60g sugar

1 tablespoon white wine vinegar

½ cup fresh orange juice

peeled rind of ½ orange, cut into thin strips

2 oz/60g mango chutney

1 Preheat oven to 400°F/200°C. To make stuffing, melt the butter in a skillet over low heat and cook the scallions for 5 minutes. Remove from the heat and stir in remaining stuffing ingredients, mixing well.

2 Pat poussin dry. Loosely pack stuffing into cavities of birds. Truss the birds, sprinkle with salt and black pepper and place on a rack in a roasting dish. Melt 1 oz/30g butter, brush over birds and roast for 30 minutes.

3 To make glaze, dissolve sugar and vinegar in a small non-reactive saucepan over moderate heat and cook until pale amber in color. Remove from heat, stir in orange juice and rind, return to heat and cook, stirring, until smooth. Stir in chutney.

4 Reduce oven to 360°F/180°C and roast birds for 15 minutes. Brush with glaze and roast for another 30 minutes or until cooked, brushing with glaze every 10 minutes. Garnish with watercress and serve.

Duck à L'Orange

serves 8

Duck à L'Orange

PREPARATION 15 mins   COOKING 1 hr 30 mins

2 x 5 lb/2½ kg ducks

peeled rind of 1 orange

salt and freshly ground

black pepper

ORANGE SAUCE

⅓ cup sugar

¼ cup sherry vinegar

1½ cups duck stock

1½ tablespoons arrowroot

½ cup port, plus 2 tablespoons

peeled rind of 2 oranges,

shredded

2 tablespoons orange-

flavored liqueur

⅔ oz/20g butter

1 To make duck stock, heat a little oil in a saucepan and brown the neck and giblets of the ducks. Pour off all fat and add 2 cups water and a bouquet garni, then gently simmer for 1 hour. Strain stock before using.

2 Meanwhile, preheat oven to 440°F/220°C. Remove excess fat from ducks, place orange rind into cavities and season to taste. Truss and place breast-side up in a roasting dish. Bake for 20 minutes or until ducks brown and release some fat. Pour off fat. Reduce oven temperature to 380°F/190°C and roast for 1 hour or until cooked.

3 To make sauce, stir sugar and vinegar in a saucepan over high heat to make a thick syrup. Remove from heat and gradually stir in stock until smooth. Return to heat and bring to the boil. Blend the arrowroot with 2 tablespoons port, then add arrowroot mixture and orange rind to the sauce and simmer until sauce thickens. Remove from heat.

4 Keep ducks warm. Remove fat from roasting dish, leaving juices in the bottom. Place dish over moderate heat, stir in remaining ½ cup port and simmer until liquid reduces by half. Strain juices into orange sauce, bring to a simmer and stir in liqueur. Season to taste, add butter and stir until melted.

5 Cut birds into serving portions, arrange on plates and glaze with some of the sauce. Serve remaining sauce separately.

serves 8–10

French Roast Stuffed Turkey

PREPARATION 1 hr 20 mins **COOKING** 2 hrs 30 mins

8 lb/4 kg turkey

2 oz/60g butter, at room temperature, plus 1 oz/30g

salt and freshly ground black pepper

4 cups chicken stock

2 tablespoons all-purpose flour

HERBED BREAD STUFFING

8 scallions, finely chopped

1 oz/30g butter

3½ oz/100g bacon pieces, chopped

4 oz/125g breadcrumbs

½ small bunch chives, chopped

3–4 sprigs thyme, leaves removed and stalks discarded

4–5 leaves sage, chopped

zest of ½ lemon

salt and freshly ground black pepper

1 egg, beaten

2 tablespoons lemon juice

RICE STUFFING

(recipe page 113)

1 Prepare rice stuffing, following the stuffing recipe on page 113.

2 To make the herbed bread stuffing, combine all dry ingredients, then add the egg and enough lemon juice to moisten. Toss with a fork – do not over-mix.

3 Preheat oven to 360°F/180°C. Carefully loosen skin from neck area and breast of turkey and loosely fill with rice stuffing. Press outside of breast to mold into shape, secure neck skin with skewers and tuck wings under body. Spoon bread stuffing into body cavity. Secure tail opening and tie legs close to body. Wipe bird dry, spread with 2 oz/60g butter and season to taste.

4 Place turkey on a rack in roasting dish and add 2 cups of the stock. Cover tightly with foil and roast for 2–2½ hours or until juices run clear when thigh is pierced with a skewer, basting every 20–25 minutes. Remove foil for the last 30 minutes of cooking to allow turkey to brown. Transfer turkey to a heated platter, cover and stand for 15 minutes before carving.

5 To make gravy, pour off all but 3 tablespoons of fat from the roasting juices. Place roasting dish over low heat, stir in 1 oz/30g butter and the flour and stir until brown. Blend in 2 cups stock. Bring to the boil, reduce heat and simmer until thickened, adding extra stock if required. Strain and serve with turkey.

Roast Goose with Nut Stuffing

Roast Goose with Nut Stuffing

PREPARATION 30 mins   **COOKING** 1 hr 50 mins

5 lb/2½ kg goose, cleaned

3 cups chicken stock

NUT STUFFING

2 oz/60g butter

2 onions, finely chopped

4 stalks celery, chopped

3 Granny Smith apples, chopped

½ teaspoon dried thyme

½ teaspoon dried sage

zest of 1 lemon

8 oz/250g breadcrumbs, made from stale bread

4 oz/125g pecans or walnuts, chopped

salt and freshly ground black pepper

1 To make stuffing, melt butter in a skillet over a moderate heat and fry onions and celery until soft. Remove from heat and combine with apples, herbs, lemon zest, breadcrumbs and nuts. Season to taste. Fill the cavity of the goose with the stuffing and fold the wings back on themselves. Sew the cavity up and tie the wings and legs against the body.

2 Preheat oven to 400°F/200°C. Season goose with salt and black pepper. Place on a rack in roasting dish and cook for 20 minutes. Drain off all fat.

3 Reduce oven to 360°F/180°C. Turn goose over so that it is breast-side down on the rack. Add 2 cups stock to dish, cover bird with a tent of foil, sealing to edge of dish, and roast for 2 hours, basting occasionally and adding more stock as needed. Remove foil and roast for 40 minutes longer or until skin is crisp and goose is cooked. Transfer to a serving platter, cover and stand for 15 minutes before carving.

Roast Goose with Spiced Apples and Figs

serves 8

Roast Goose with Spiced Apples and Figs

PREPARATION 30 mins　COOKING 2 hrs 45 mins

2 oz/60g butter

1 large onion, chopped

13 oz/375g dried figs, chopped

6 oz/180g fresh breadcrumbs

1 egg

¼ cup parsley, chopped

8 sprigs thyme, leaves removed and stalks discarded

salt and freshly ground black pepper

10-12 lb/5–6 kg oven-ready goose

1 small loaf of bread

8 small apples

16 whole cloves

1 oz/30g light muscovado sugar

½ teaspoon ground mixed spice

1 Preheat oven to 360°F/180°C. Melt 1 oz/30g of the butter in a saucepan. Add onion and fry for 3 minutes. Remove from heat and add 8 oz/250g of the figs, the breadcrumbs, egg, parsley and thyme. Season lightly with salt and pepper and mix well together.

2 Pack half the stuffing into the neck end of the goose. Tuck flap of skin under bird and truss – fold the wings under the body and tie the legs together with string. Place goose on a rack standing over a roasting dish.

3 Remove crust from loaf of bread and push bread into body cavity of bird to absorb fat during roasting. Cook goose in the oven for 2¾ hours.

4 Meanwhile, core apples and cut a thin slice off top of each. Stud each apple with 2 whole cloves. Stand in a roasting dish. Mix the remaining figs with the sugar and mixed spice and pack into apples, letting excess stuffing rest on top. Melt remaining butter and pour over apples.

5 Thirty minutes before the goose is ready, place apples in oven, basting frequently.

6 To test if goose is cooked, pierce thickest part of thigh with a skewer – the juices should run clear. Transfer goose to a warmed serving platter.

Note Yorkshire puddings (recipe page 108) are a wonderful accompaniment to the spiced apples.

Roast Rib of Beef

Roast Rib of Beef

PREPARATION 25 mins   COOKING 50 mins

6-point standing rib roast, about 3 lb/1½ kg

salt and freshly ground black pepper

HERBED PIQUANT SAUCE

6 scallions, finely chopped

1 very small clove garlic, chopped

3 tablespoons dry white wine

1 tablespoon wine vinegar

8 oz/250g butter, at room temperature

¼ cup parsley, chopped

¼ cup chervil, chopped

1 teaspoon lemon juice

1 teaspoon salt

freshly ground black pepper

ground nutmeg

1 Preheat oven to 400°F/200°C. Rub roast all over with salt and black pepper. Place on a rack fat-side up in a roasting dish and roast for 50 minutes.

2 To make sauce, place scallions, garlic, wine and vinegar in a small saucepan. Bring to the boil and boil for 2 minutes or until reduced to 1 tablespoon. Cool slightly, then gradually whisk in butter until blended and creamy, like mayonnaise. Stir in herbs, lemon juice, salt, black pepper and nutmeg to taste. Place in a sauce boat and set in a pan of warm water to keep warm.

3 To serve, place beef fat-side down on a carving board and remove ribs by cutting close down the line of bones. Cut ribs apart and set aside. Turn roast upright and carve slices from one end, arranging them around the roast for serving. Serve beef with the ribs, pan juices and sauce.

serves 6

Salsa Rib Roast

PREPARATION 20 mins   **COOKING** 50 mins

6-point standing rib roast
of beef, about 3 lb/1½ kg

salt and freshly ground
black pepper

2 cloves garlic, crushed

2 tablespoons all-purpose flour

TOMATO SALSA

8 plum tomatoes,
finely chopped

1 medium red onion,
finely chopped

10 leaves basil, chopped

sprinkle of garlic bread
seasoning

salt

1 tablespoon olive oil

1½ tablespoons balsamic
dressing

1 Preheat oven to 400°F/200°C. Rub the roast with salt, pepper and crushed garlic. Just before placing in the oven, dust all over with flour – this helps to seal in the juices. Place in the oven and cook for 50 minutes until medium rare (cook for a further 15 minutes for well done).

2 Meanwhile, combine all salsa ingredients in a small saucepan ready for heating. Remove the roast from the oven and rest the meat for 5 minutes. Warm the salsa while the meat rests.

Stuffed Lamb Roast with Orange

serves 4

1 Combine all stuffing ingredients in a bowl and set aside. Preheat oven to 360°F/180°C and line a small baking dish with baking paper. Make a small pocket in each mini lamb roast with a sharp knife.

2 Place some of the stuffing in each of the lamb roasts and secure with a metal skewer or toothpicks. Brush olive oil over each roast and bake for 30 minutes. Wrap in foil to rest, reserving the pan juices in the baking dish.

3 Place the baking dish on the stovetop over a low heat and add the cream and quarter of the orange juice and stir until combined, then add the garlic and the rest of the orange juice and season to taste. Reduce the sauce until thick and creamy. Serve the sauce over the top of the roasts.

2 mini lamb roasts

1 tablespoon extra-virgin olive oil

½ cup heavy cream

juice of 1 orange

1 clove garlic

salt and freshly ground black pepper

STUFFING

1 orange, peeled and segmented

¼ cup hazelnuts, chopped

3 scallions, sliced

zest of 1 orange

¼ small bunch tarragon, leaves removed and stalks discarded

¾ cup fresh breadcrumbs

1 oz/30g butter, melted

Every headliner needs a support act, so in addition to the roasts, there needs to be a range of tasty side treats to choose from. Savoury side dishes help dress the table with wonderful colours, smells and flavours, and are the perfect accompaniment for roasts, seafood banquets or vegetable bakes – whatever style of Christmas you are having this year. With these recipes, don't be too surprised if the headliner gets a little upstaged by the supporting cast!

All the Trimmings

COLLECTORS EDITION

All the Trimmings

COLLECTORS EDITION

Beetroot Horseradish Pickle

makes 2 lb/1 kg

PREPARATION 15 mins   COOKING 45 mins

2 lb/1 kg beetroot

1 oz/60g horseradish relish

4 oz/125g sugar

2½ cups wine vinegar

1 teaspoon salt

½ teaspoon fennel seeds

6 juniper berries

1 In a large pot of water, boil the beetroot for 30 minutes, cool then peel. If they are large, cut into wedges, if small leave whole. Mix together beetroot and horseradish relish and pack into hot, sterilized jars.

2 Meanwhile place sugar, vinegar, salt, fennel seeds and juniper berries into a saucepan and simmer for 15 minutes. Pour hot mixture over beetroot and seal. Store in refrigerator for 8–10 days to allow flavors to develop before eating.

Cranberry Ginger Relish

makes 750g

Cranberry Ginger Relish

PREPARATION 5 mins COOKING 15 mins

1 lb/500g fresh or frozen cranberries

zest of 1 large orange

¾ cup fresh orange juice

½ cup maple syrup

3 in/8cm piece ginger, finely chopped

1 Place all ingredients in a large saucepan and bring to the boil over medium heat. Reduce heat and simmer gently, stirring occasionally, for 10–15 minutes or until berries pop open. Cool.

2 Store in covered jars in refrigerator for at least 1 week to allow flavors to mature.

Note If you can only get dried cranberries, soak them overnight in cranberry juice and 1 tablespoon of sugar.

Spiced Red Cabbage

Spiced Red Cabbage

PREPARATION 20 mins   **COOKING** 1 hr 30 mins

1½ lb/750g red cabbage

1 large red onion, chopped

1 green apple, cored and chopped

2 cloves garlic, crushed

¼ teaspoon ground cloves

¼ teaspoon ground nutmeg

1½ tablespoons Demerara sugar

2 tablespoons red wine vinegar

1 oz/30g butter, cut into ⅓ in/1cm cubes

salt and freshly ground black pepper

1 Preheat the oven to 300°F/150°C. Cut the cabbage into quarters and remove the white core. Finely slice the leaves and add to a large ovenproof dish, then add the onion and apple and toss to combine.

2 In a small bowl, combine the garlic, spices, sugar and vinegar. Pour the mixture over the cabbage, and toss to combine again. Distribute the butter cubes across the top evenly. Cover and bake for 1½ hours, stirring once after the first hour. Season and serve hot.

Minted Peas

PREPARATION 5 mins   COOKING 6 mins

4 cups fresh or frozen peas

5 whole sprigs mint, plus

5 sprigs with stalks removed
and leaves shredded

1½ oz/45g butter

salt

white pepper

1 Place the peas in a saucepan and pour in enough water to just cover. Add the whole mint sprigs. Bring to the boil and simmer for 5 minutes if fresh, 2 minutes if frozen.

2 Meanwhile, in a small saucepan over a low heat, melt the butter and add the shredded mint to infuse.

3 When the peas are cooked, drain and discard the mint. Return peas to the saucepan, add the butter and shredded mint and stir over a low heat until combined. Season with salt and white pepper.

serves 6

Broccolini
with Almonds

PREPARATION 5 mins   COOKING 10 mins

1 lb/500g broccolini,
stalks trimmed

2 teaspoons olive oil

¾ oz/20g butter

1 clove garlic, crushed

2 tablespoons flaked almonds

1 Add the broccolini to a saucepan of boiling water and cook for 1–2 minutes or until still just crunchy. Drain well.

2 Heat the oil and butter in a large skillet, add the garlic and almonds and cook for 1–2 minutes, or until the almonds are just golden. Remove the almonds from the skillet with a slotted spoon and set aside.

3 Add the broccolini to the skillet and toss over medium heat for 2–3 minutes until the broccolini is heated through and well coated. Return the almonds to the skillet and stir until well distributed. Serve hot.

Cajun Potato Cakes

PREPARATION 15 mins **COOKING** 8 mins

4 medium potatoes, boiled
in their jackets

2 eggs, lightly beaten

2 teaspoons Cajun seasoning

2 tablespoons olive oil

8 tablespoons all-purpose flour

½ teaspoon salt

1 Skin the boiled potatoes and mash well. Add eggs, Cajun seasoning, olive oil, flour and salt. Mix well and form into 16 patties with floured hands.

2 Lightly oil a skillet and cook the cakes for about 4 minutes on each side.

makes 20

Duchess Potatoes

PREPARATION 30 mins   COOKING 40 mins

3 oz/850g potatoes, peeled
and quartered

2 eggs, plus 1 egg yolk

¼ cup heavy cream

⅔ oz/20g Parmesan cheese,
grated

¼ teaspoon grated nutmeg

salt

white pepper

¼ teaspoon smoked paprika

1 In a large pot full of cold water, bring the potatoes to the boil and cook for 20 minutes or until very tender. Drain and return potatoes to the pot. Turn the heat to very low and shake the pan for 1–2 minutes to dry out the potatoes. Remove from the heat and mash until smooth.

2 Beat together the eggs, cream, cheese, nutmeg, salt, white pepper and a pinch of the paprika. Add to the potato and mash to combine. Adjust seasoning if necessary. Cover loosely and leave for 15 minutes to cool slightly.

3 Preheat oven to 360°F/180°C and lightly butter a baking tray. Fill a piping bag fitted with a ½ in/15mm star nozzle with the warm potato mixture. Pipe mixture into swirls on the baking tray, leaving room between each mound. Lightly brush all over with the egg yolk and bake for 15–20 minutes until golden. Serve hot, sprinkled with the remaining paprika.

Note These can be prepared ahead of time and refrigerated. Just before serving, brush with egg yolk and bake.

Roast Potatoes with Garlic and Rosemary

serves 8

Roast Potatoes with Garlic and Rosemary

PREPARATION 15 mins   **COOKING** 1 hr 15 mins

3 lb/1½ kg chat potatoes

coarse sea salt

1 bulb garlic

6 sprigs rosemary, leaves removed and chopped

6 tablespoons olive oil

1 Preheat oven to 380°F/190°C. Place potatoes in a saucepan, cover with water, add salt and bring to the boil. Reduce heat and simmer for 2 minutes, then drain well. Make a few cuts across the tops of the potatoes. Break open the garlic and discard any loose pieces of skin.

2 Place potatoes and garlic cloves in a roasting dish, sprinkle with the chopped rosemary and oil. Bake for about 1¼ hours, turning occasionally, until crisp and golden brown. Transfer to a warmed serving dish, sprinkle with salt and garnish with extra rosemary sprigs.

serves 8

Bourbon
Sweet Potatoes

PREPARATION 10 mins   COOKING 45 mins

2 lb/1 kg orange sweet
potatoes, peeled and
cut into even-size pieces

1 oz/30g butter

1 tablespoon vegetable oil

1 tablespoon honey

2 tablespoons Bourbon

pinch of ground ginger

6 fresh sage leaves torn
into pieces

1 Preheat oven to 360°F/180°C. Cook
sweet potatoes in a large saucepan of
boiling salted water for 5 minutes. Drain.
Melt the butter with the oil in a baking
dish and stir in honey, Bourbon and ginger.
Add the sage and the sweet potatoes
and toss in mixture to coat.

2 Bake for 40 minutes, brushing with
honey mixture and turning occasionally,
until potatoes are tender. Garnish with
extra sage.

serves 4

Cauliflower Cheese

PREPARATION 15 mins   COOKING 20 mins

1 lb/500g cauliflower, cut into small pieces

¼ cup fresh breadcrumbs

¼ small bunch flat-leaf parsley

CHEESE SAUCE

1 oz/30g butter

1 oz/30g all-purpose flour

1¼ cups milk, warmed

1 teaspoon wholegrain mustard

3 oz/90g Parmesan cheese, grated, at room temperature

salt

white pepper

1 Lightly butter a 6 cup heatproof dish. Cook the cauliflower in a saucepan of lightly salted boiling water for 8 minutes or until just tender. Drain thoroughly, then transfer to the prepared dish and keep warm.

2 To make the cheese sauce, melt the butter in a saucepan over low heat. Stir in the flour and cook for 1 minute, or until lightly colored and bubbling. Remove from the heat and gradually stir in the milk and mustard. If lumps form, press the mixture through a strainer. Return to the heat and stir constantly until the sauce simmers and thickens. Reduce the heat and simmer for a further 2 minutes, then remove from the heat again. Add the Parmesan and stir until thoroughly combined. Season with salt and white pepper and pour over the cauliflower.

3 Combine the breadcrumbs and parsley and sprinkle evenly on top of the sauce. Grill under a medium heat until the top is golden brown. Serve immediately.

PREPARATION 15 mins   **COOKING** 25 mins

4 eggs

¾ cup milk

2 cups all-purpose flour

1 teaspoon salt

¼ small bunch parsley, chopped

¼ small bunch chives, chopped

½ cup vegetable oil

1 Combine the eggs and milk thoroughly with a fork (do not whisk). Using a whisk to combine, add enough of the flour to form a thick but pourable batter. Add salt to taste, then the chopped herbs.

2 Preheat oven to 400°F/200°C. In a 12-cup muffin tray, add 2 teaspoons of oil to each muffin mold and place in the oven for 15 minutes. When both the molds and oil are hot, pour in the batter – if it does not start to sizzle immediately, stop and return molds to the oven until hot enough.

3 Place on the middle shelf and bake for about 25 minutes until risen, golden brown and slightly crisp – an empty tray on the top shelf will help prevent them browning too much. Remove from the oven, carefully remove from the molds and serve immediately.

It's important to remember that not everybody chooses or is able to eat the same things, so we have put together some recipes that will help you prepare for guests who are vegetarian, vegan or have wheat allergies. However, there's no need to wait for a vegetarian to come to dinner to make these delicious recipes – we recommend you make them part of your regular Christmas menu, both for variety and balance.

Special Guests

COLLECTORS EDITION

Special Guests

COLLECTORS EDITION

Roasted Vegetable Frittata

serves 6

PREPARATION 15 mins   **COOKING** 50 mins

½ cup sour cream

¼ cup milk

2 oz/60g Parmesan cheese, grated

8 oz/250g baby potatoes, cut into ¼ in/5mm slices

4 oz/250g sweet potatoes, peeled and cut into ¼ in/5mm slices

2½ tablespoons olive oil

salt and freshly ground black pepper

1 large courgette, halved and sliced

1 red pepper, deseeded and diced

1 leek, trimmed, halved, washed and sliced

1 clove garlic, crushed

2 teaspoons Italian herbs

6 eggs, lightly beaten

1 Preheat the oven to 440°F/220°C. Place the potatoes and sweet potatoes in a non-stick baking tray. Drizzle over 1½ tablespoons of oil and season with salt and pepper. Toss to combine and bake for 10 minutes, turning from time to time. Add the courgette and red pepper and bake for a further 15 minutes, turning from time to time.

2 Heat the remaining oil in a 9 in/23cm non-stick heavy-based skillet over medium heat. Cook the leek and garlic for 3–4 minutes. Stir in the Italian herbs, then add the roasted vegetables and toss to combine.

3 Whisk together the eggs, sour cream, milk, and Parmesan cheese. Pour the egg mixture over the vegetables. Reduce the heat to low and cook for 12–15 minutes or until nearly cooked.

4 Place the skillet under a hot broiler for 4–5 minutes or until golden and cooked. Place a kitchen towel around the handle before removing from the broiler. Cut the frittata into wedges and serve with crusty bread and salad.

Note Suitable for vegetarians and wheat allergy sufferers.

serves 4

Tomato, Mustard and Brie Tart

PREPARATION 45 mins   COOKING 50 mins

6 oz/175g all-purpose flour

sea salt and freshly ground black pepper

2½ oz/75g butter, diced

½ cup milk

2 medium egg yolks

1 clove garlic, crushed

1 tablespoon wholegrain mustard

2 oz/60g aged Cheddar, grated

4 ripe tomatoes, sliced

4 oz/125g Dutch Brie, thinly sliced

¼ cup basil, finely shredded

¼ cup parsley, finely chopped

¼ cup cilantro, finely chopped

2 tablespoons extra-virgin olive oil

1 Sift the flour and a pinch of sea salt into a bowl, then rub the butter in, using your fingertips, until it resembles fine breadcrumbs. Add 2 tablespoons of cold water and mix to a dough. Cover and refrigerate for 20 minutes. Use the pastry to line a deep 8 in/20cm metal flan dish and chill for a further 10 minutes.

2 Preheat the oven to 380°F/190°C. Prick the pastry base lightly with a fork, then line with baking paper. Half-fill with dried beans or rice and bake 'blind' for 10–12 minutes. Carefully remove the paper and beans and bake the pastry for a further 5 minutes. Set aside, then reduce the oven temperature to 360°F/180°C.

3 In a jug, beat together the milk, egg yolks and garlic and season to taste. Spread the mustard over the base of the pastry and sprinkle over the Cheddar. Arrange the tomatoes and Brie on top and pour over the egg mixture. Bake for 30–35 minutes, until just set and golden.

4 Mix together the basil, parsley, cilantro and oil and drizzle over the tart. Serve warm.

Note Suitable for vegetarians.

Baby Peppers with Wild Rice

serves 4

Baby Peppers with Wild Rice

PREPARATION 25 mins   COOKING 1 hr 15 mins

¼ cup olive oil

⅔ cup slivered almonds

1 small onion, chopped

1 stalk celery, chopped

½ cup wild rice, rinsed

1 cup raisins

½ teaspoon dried marjoram

1 bunch fresh parsley, chopped

¼ teaspoon ground nutmeg

1 teaspoon salt

¼ teaspoon black pepper

½ cup long-grain rice

3½ oz/100g spinach, chopped

2 tablespoons rice flour

12 baby red peppers, cut in half

1 Heat oil in a large saucepan over medium heat. Add almonds and stir until golden. Lift out with a slotted spoon and set aside. Add onion and celery to pan and stir-fry for 5 minutes. Add wild rice, raisins, herbs, spices and 2½ cups water. Bring to a boil, reduce heat, season, cover and simmer for 25 minutes.

2 Add long-grain rice and stir to combine. Continue cooking gently until most of the water has been absorbed and rice is tender, about 25 minutes. Add spinach, toss and cover, then simmer for 2 minutes. Remove from heat and, when cool, stir in almonds and rice flour.

3 Preheat oven to 360°F/180°C. Remove the seeds and any white membrane from the red peppers and stuff with the rice stuffing. Cook for 15 minutes and serve warm.

Note This is suitable for vegetarians, vegans and wheat allergy sufferers, and works perfectly as a stuffing for poultry as well as vegetables.

makes 30

Cheese Almond Shortbreads

PREPARATION 1 hr 10 mins   **COOKING** 15 mins

4 oz/125g aged Parmesan
cheese, finely grated,
at room temperature

6 oz/180g butter, at room
temperature

¾ cup rice flour

¼ cup almond meal

1 teaspoon salt

¼ teaspoon freshly ground
black pepper

3 tablespoons almonds,
finely chopped

pinch of Cayenne pepper

¼ small bunch basil, chopped

7 oz/200g mascarpone
cheese

1 Beat Parmesan and butter until creamy. Add flour and almond meal, then salt and black pepper and stir into creamed mixture. Add almonds, then add Cayenne and fold to combine evenly.

2 Flour your hands and shape the dough into a ball, then divide in half and place each half on a large sheet of plastic wrap. Roll each dough into a neat cylinder shape 1½ in/4cm in diameter, wrap around the plastic wrap and twist the ends to firm up the shape (finished dough will look like a Christmas bon bon). Refrigerate for 1 hour.

3 Preheat oven to 360°F/180°C and line 2 oven trays with baking paper. Unwrap the dough and cut into ¼ in/5mm-thick slices with a sharp knife. Place the slices 2 in/5cm apart on the trays and bake for 12–15 minutes. Cool completely.

4 Meanwhile fold the basil through the mascarpone, then season with more black pepper. Put 1 teaspoon on each shortbread and top with extra basil leaves.

Note Suitable for vegetarians and wheat allergy sufferers.

Mushroom Nut Roast with Tomato Sauce

serves 6

Mushroom Nut Roast with Tomato Sauce

PREPARATION 30 mins   **COOKING** 1 hr

2 tablespoons olive oil

1 large onion, diced

2 cloves garlic, crushed

10 oz/300g mushrooms, finely chopped

7 oz/200g cashews

7 oz/200g Brazil nuts

3 oz/90g Cheddar cheese, grated

1 oz/30g Parmesan cheese, grated

1 egg, lightly beaten

¼ small bunch chives, chopped

½ cup instant polenta

salt and freshly ground black pepper

TOMATO SAUCE

1½ tablespoons olive oil

1 onion, finely chopped

1 clove garlic, crushed

17 oz/400g canned chopped tomatoes

1 tablespoon tomato purée

½ teaspoon brown sugar

1 Butter a 5 x 8 in/14 x 21cm loaf tin and line with baking paper. Heat the oil in a skillet and add the onion, garlic and mushrooms. Fry until soft, then cool.

2 Process the nuts in a food processor until finely chopped, but do not over-blend.

3 Preheat the oven to 360°F/180°C. Combine the cooled mushrooms, chopped nuts, Cheddar, Parmesan, egg, chives and polenta in a bowl. Mix well and season to taste. Press into the loaf tin and bake for 45 minutes.

4 Meanwhile, prepare the tomato sauce. Heat the oil in a saucepan over a medium heat, add the onion and garlic and cook for 4 minutes, stirring 2–3 times. Stir in the tomatoes, tomato purée, sugar and ⅓ cup water. Simmer gently for 5 minutes.

5 When cooked, remove loaf from the oven and leave for 5 minutes, then gently turn out, cool for a further 2 minutes and cut into slices. Season with salt and pepper and serve with the tomato sauce.

Note Suitable for vegetarians and wheat allergy sufferers.

Lemon and Rosemary Baked Ricotta

serves 4

Lemon and Rosemary Baked Ricotta

PREPARATION 4 hrs   COOKING 30 mins

2 lb/1 kg fresh ricotta

5 oz/150g cherry tomatoes, halved

½ cup extra-virgin olive oil, plus 1 tablespoon

salt and freshly ground black pepper

zest and juice of 1 lemon

1 clove garlic, crushed

1 sprig rosemary, leaves removed and chopped

¼ cup fresh basil leaves

¼ cup fresh parsley leaves

1 Place the ricotta in a sieve lined with muslin cloth, press into the shape of the sieve, cover and refrigerate for 4 hours.

2 Meanwhile, preheat oven to 360°F/180°C. Place the tomatoes on an oven tray, drizzle over 1 tablespoon oil and season with salt and pepper. Roast for 10 minutes, remove from the oven and cool on a wire rack.

3 Mix ¼ cup of oil with the lemon zest, juice and garlic and set aside.

4 Remove ricotta from the seive, place onto a lined baking tray and drizzle with the remaining oil. Sprinkle with the rosemary, season with salt and pepper and bake until golden, about 20 minutes.

5 Add the tomatoes, basil and parsley to the lemon dressing, mix together and serve over the baked ricotta.

Note Suitable for vegetarians and wheat allergy sufferers.

serves 4

Polenta and Corn Fritters

PREPARATION 25 mins   COOKING 15 mins

½ teaspoon salt

½ cup instant polenta

¼ cup corn kernels

¼ red pepper, diced

1 scallion, finely sliced

¼ cup parsley, finely chopped

1 small clove garlic, minced

⅓ cup rice flour

¼ teaspoon baking powder

1 egg, lightly beaten

salt and freshly ground

black pepper

2 tablespoons olive oil

CREMA VERDE

¼ cup heavy cream

¼ cup sour cream

1 tablespoon pesto

½ small bunch flat-leaf parsley,

finely shredded

1 teaspoon lemon juice

salt and freshly ground

black pepper

1 In a saucepan, bring 1½ cups water and the salt to a boil, gradually add polenta, stirring continuously for 3–5 minutes until the polenta thickens and begins to come away from the sides of the pan. Remove from the heat and add corn, red pepper, scallion, parsley and garlic. Stir until combined. Transfer to a bowl and leave to cool.

2 Sift flour and baking powder together and combine with polenta mixture. Add egg and salt and pepper. Heat oil in a skillet over a medium-high heat, and place tablespoonfuls of mixture in the skillet. Cook for 1–2 minutes on each side.

3 To make the crema verde, place all ingredients in a bowl and mix together until smooth. Serve fritters with crema verde at the side.

Note Suitable for vegetarians and wheat allergy sufferers.

Pumpkin Risotto in Golden Nuggets

makes 4

Pumpkin Risotto in Golden Nuggets

PREPARATION 20 mins   **COOKING** 50 mins

5 golden nugget pumpkins

1 tablespoon olive oil

4 cups vegetable stock

salt and freshly ground black pepper

2½ oz/75g butter

1 small onion, finely chopped

1¼ cups Arborio rice

⅔ oz/20g Parmesan cheese, grated

1 Preheat the oven to 380°F/190°C. Peel and grate 1 pumpkin and set aside. Wash and dry the remaining pumpkins, cut the cap off each and scoop out the seeds. Rinse the seeds and place on a baking tray. Rub the pumpkins with the oil. Place on the baking tray with the seeds and bake for 10 minutes. Remove the seeds, then continue baking the pumpkins for a further 30–40 minutes, until tender when pierced with a skewer.

2 Meanwhile, cook the risotto. Bring the stock to the boil in a saucepan, season with salt and pepper and leave gently simmering. In another pan, heat 2 oz/60g of the butter and cook the onion and grated pumpkin until softened. Add the rice to the saucepan and cook over a medium heat, stirring constantly, for 3 minutes or until rice becomes translucent. Pour 1 cup hot stock into rice mixture and cook, stirring constantly, until liquid is absorbed. Continue cooking in this way until all the stock is used and the rice is tender. Remove the pan from the heat and stir in the remaining butter and grated Parmesan.

3 Fill each pumpkin with the risotto and serve immediately, garnished with the roasted pumpkin seeds and a few small sage leaves.

Note Suitable for vegetarians and wheat allergy sufferers.

Vegan Moussaka

serves 6

Vegan Moussaka

PREPARATION 1 hr   COOKING 1 hr

TOMATO SAUCE

1 eggplant, thinly sliced

2 courgette, thinly sliced

2½ tablespoons olive oil

1 large carrot, diced

1 stalk celery, diced

1 leek, sliced and well washed

1 large onion, diced

2 cloves garlic, crushed

14 oz/400g canned tomatoes

½ cup red wine

¼ cup fresh basil

1 teaspoon dried oregano

salt and freshly ground

black pepper

7 oz/200g vegan cheese

BÉCHAMEL SAUCE

1 tablespoon cornstarch

4 cups soymilk

1 tablespoon olive oil

1 small onion, halved

freshly ground black pepper

½ teaspoon soy sauce

freshly grated nutmeg

1 Preheat oven to 360°F/180°C. Coat the eggplant and courgette with 2 tablespoons olive oil. Place on 2 baking sheets and bake for 10 minutes, turning once. Set aside to cool.

2 Meanwhile, add remaining oil to a skillet and fry the carrot, celery, leek and onion for 10 minutes, stirring often. Add the garlic, tomatoes, red wine, basil and oregano and simmer for 20 minutes.

3 In a rectangular baking dish, place a layer of eggplant, then a layer of sauce, then a layer of half eggplant and half courgette. Cover this with another layer of sauce then finish off with the remaining courgette.

4 To make the béchamel, place the cornstarch in a bowl, add a little of the milk and mix to a paste. Heat the remaining milk in a pan, stirring constantly. Just before boiling, pour into the bowl with the cornstarch mixture, making sure to keep stirring. Return to the milk pan and stir constantly for 2 minutes. Lower the heat, add the oil, onion, ground pepper and soy sauce. Keep stirring on a low heat for 5 minutes.

5 Preheat the oven to 400°F/200°C. Grate some nutmeg into the sauce, remove the onion then pour over the moussaka. Scatter with the cheese and bake for 10 minutes covered and another 20 minutes uncovered.

Note Suitable for vegetarians, vegans and wheat allergy sufferers.

serves 4

Potato and Tomato Pie

PREPARATION 15 mins   COOKING 40 mins

3 cups vegetable stock

1½ lb/750g potatoes, peeled and thinly sliced

1 red pepper

6 plum tomatoes, sliced

2 tablespoons lemon juice

2 tablespoons olive oil

¼ teaspoon sugar

freshly ground black pepper

¼ small bunch flat-leaf parsley, chopped

¼ small bunch cilantro, chopped

1 Heat vegetable stock in a large skillet over medium heat. Add potatoes and cook for 8–10 minutes or until tender. Drain potatoes, reserving ½ cup stock, and rinse under cold water.

2 Cut red pepper into four and remove seeds. Place on a baking tray and bake under a hot grill for 6-8 minutes or until skin blisters. Leave to cool then remove skin and slice thinly.

3 Preheat oven to 440°F/220°C and lightly butter a shallow casserole dish. Arrange potato slices and red pepper in the casserole dish. Pour over reserved stock and arrange tomato slices on top. Drizzle with lemon juice and olive oil, then sprinkle with sugar and season with pepper.

4 Bake for 20 minutes or until tomatoes are cooked. Garnish with parsley and cilantro to serve.

Note Suitable for vegetarians, vegans and wheat allergy sufferers.

Courgette Polenta Slices

serves 4

1 Lightly oil a shallow 8 in/22cm square roasting dish. Heat half the oil in a large skillet. Fry the courgette for 3–4 minutes, stirring frequently, until softened but not browned. Remove from the heat.

2 Bring the stock to the boil in a large saucepan. Sprinkle in the polenta, stirring with a wooden spoon, and continue to stir for 5 minutes or until the polenta thickens and begins to come away from the sides of the pan. Remove from the heat and stir in the courgette. Season to taste.

3 Tip the polenta into the roasting dish, spreading evenly, then sprinkle with cheese and leave for 1 hour to cool and set. Cut the polenta into slices, brush with the rest of the oil and cook under a preheated broiler for 2–4 minutes on each side until golden.

3 tablespoons olive oil

8 oz/250g courgette, grated

3 cups vegetable stock

6 oz/175g instant polenta

salt and freshly ground black pepper

2 oz/60g vegan cheese, finely grated

Note Suitable for vegetarians, vegans and wheat allergy sufferers.

Christmas baking is a tradition with a very long and distinguished history. Many of these desserts, cakes and baked treats are only prepared at this special time of year, which only adds to their appeal. We all have strong memories of waking early, unwrapping presents and spending time with family, all the time with delicious smells from the kitchen wafting through the house. Now you can continue the tradition by making family favourites such as Christmas cake, fruit mince pies or Christmas pudding.

Christmas
Baking

Christmas
Baking

COLLECTORS EDITION

PREPARATION 10 mins   COOKING 30 mins

2 oz/60g butter

2 oz/60g soft light brown sugar

⅓ cup corn syrup

1 teaspoon ground ginger

¼ cup all-purpose flour, sifted

zest of 1 lemon

2 teaspoons lemon juice

1¼ cups heavy cream, whipped

1 Preheat oven to 440°F/220°C. Place butter, sugar, corn syrup and ginger in a saucepan over low heat and stir until butter melts and sugar dissolves. Cool slightly, add flour, lemon zest and juice and mix well.

2 Line two baking sheets with non-stick baking paper. On one sheet, drop generous teaspoons of mixture in 5 mounds, 4 in/10cm apart, and bake for 12–15 minutes or until mounds spread out to form lacy, malleable rounds.

3 Cool briefly, remove with a palette knife and quickly roll around handle of a wooden spoon. Allow to set, then carefully slip off spoon and cool. While rolling one batch, bake the next. Store in an airtight container. Just prior to serving, fill with whipped cream.

makes 12

Perfect Christmas Cupcakes

PREPARATION 20 mins   COOKING 20 mins

5 oz/150g all-purpose flour

1 teaspoon baking powder

½ teaspoon baking soda

1 teaspoon ground mixed spice

pinch of salt

3½ oz/100g sweet butter, at room temperature

5½ oz/160g dark brown sugar

2 large eggs

3 tablespoons sour cream

2½ oz/75g dark chocolate, broken into pieces

1 teaspoon instant coffee

36 dried cranberries

ICING

1½ cups confectioner's sugar

1 egg white

½ teaspoon lemon juice

1 Preheat the oven to 400°F/200°C and place a cupcake paper into each cup of a 12-cup muffin tray. In a large mixing bowl, combine the flour, baking powder, baking soda, mixed spice and salt. In a separate bowl, cream the butter and sugar, then add the eggs one at a time. Add half the flour mixture, followed by half the sour cream, then repeat.

2 In a medium saucepan over a medium-low heat, combine ½ cup boiling water with the chocolate and instant coffee. Heat until the chocolate just melts, cool slightly, then fold into the cake batter using a spatula – this will create a thin batter. Pour into the paper cases and bake for 20 minutes.

3 Meanwhile, prepare the icing. Sift the confectioner's sugar through a fine sieve. Using a wooden spoon in a small bowl, lightly beat the egg white. Slowly add the sugar one heaped tablespoon at a time (through the sieve again), beating thoroughly after each addition.

4 When all of the sugar is completely mixed, add the lemon juice and beat for another minute. Remove the cupcakes from the oven, cool in the tray for 5 minutes, then place on a wire rack until completely cold.

7 Cover the tops of the cupcakes with a thick layer of the icing and top with the dried cranberries.

Christmas Mince Pies

makes 12

Christmas Mince Pies

PREPARATION 1 hr 50 mins   COOKING 25 mins

FRUIT MINCE

8 oz/250g shredded suet

2 oz/60g blanched almonds,
finely chopped

4 oz/125g candied peel,
finely chopped

1 Granny Smith apple,
peeled and chopped

2 oz/60g glacé cherries,
chopped

2 oz/60g glacé ginger,
chopped

1½ lb/750g mixed dried fruit

8 oz/250g soft brown sugar

¼ teaspoon salt

¼ teaspoon ground nutmeg

¼ teaspoon ground mixed
spice

juice and zest of 1 orange

juice and zest of 1 lemon

½ cup brandy or rum

1 egg, beaten

SHORTCRUST PASTRY

1¾ cups all-purpose flour

½ teaspoon salt

6 oz/180g butter, cut into
pieces

1 tablespoon superfine sugar

1 egg yolk

1 To make the fruit mince, remove any fibres from suet and mix with almonds, peel and apple. Add cherries, ginger and mixed fruit and mix to combine.

2 Coarsely mince two-thirds of the fruit mixture. Combine remaining third with the minced mixture, then stir in sugar, salt, spices, citrus zests and juices, and brandy or rum.

3 To make pastry, sift flour and salt into a bowl. Rub in butter with fingertips until mixture resembles breadcrumbs. Stir in the sugar and make a well in the center. Blend the egg yolk with 2 tablespoons iced water, add to the flour and mix to make a dough. Knead lightly on a floured surface until smooth. Wrap and chill for 1 hour.

4 Preheat oven to 380°F/190°C and lightly butter 12 small patty tins. Roll out the pastry thinly into a rectangle. Cut out 12 rounds to fit the patty tins, and 12 stars to decorate the tops.

5 Fill pastry cases with fruit mince and cover with pastry stars. Brush with beaten egg and sprinkle with extra superfine sugar.

6 Bake for 25 minutes or until golden. Stand briefly in tins before turning out. Serve warm or cold.

Note Any leftover fruit mince can be packed into sterilized jars, covered with circles of baking paper dipped in brandy, then covered with lids to seal.

Sugared Pears

serves 4

Sugared Pears

PREPARATION 15 mins   COOKING 1 hr 15 mins

4 almost-ripe pears, halved and cored

130g superfine sugar

4 egg yolks

1 cup heavy cream, scalded

2 tablespoons brandy

½ teaspoon ground ginger

1 Preheat oven to 360°F/180°C and lightly butter a 10 in/25cm round ovenproof dish. Slice pear halves at ¼ in/5mm intervals, but keep them attached at the top. Arrange, cut-side down, in the dish and open into fan shapes.

2 Add ⅓ cup water to dish and sprinkle pears with half the sugar. Bake until tender and lightly caramelized, covering with baking paper or foil if they color too quickly.

3 Meanwhile, beat egg yolks and remaining sugar until pale. Gradually whisk hot cream into egg mixture. Return to saucepan and stir over low heat until thickened. Whisk until lukewarm. Stir in brandy and ginger, cover and set aside. When pears are cooked, serve with the brandy custard.

Iced Plum Cream in Wafer Cups

serves 8

Iced Plum Cream in Wafer Cups

PREPARATION 2 hrs 20 mins   **COOKING** 30 mins

¼ cup orange-flavored

liqueur or rum

3 oz/90g pitted prunes, diced

2 oz/60g dried apricots,

chopped

4 cups vanilla ice cream,

slightly softened

2 oz/60g butter

2½ oz/75g superfine sugar

½ cup corn syrup

⅓ cup all-purpose flour, sifted

1 teaspoon ground ginger

1 oz/30g walnuts or pecans,

chopped

1 Heat liqueur or rum until warm, add prunes and apricots and soak for 30 minutes. Fold mixture into ice cream, cover and freeze until ready to serve.

2 To make wafer cups, melt butter, sugar and corn syrup in a saucepan over low heat until combined. Cool to lukewarm. Stir in flour and ginger, then nuts.

3 Preheat oven to 360°F/180°C and lightly butter two baking sheets. Drop mixture in 2–3 tablespoonfuls onto the trays, allowing room for spreading. Bake one tray at a time for 10 minutes or until golden, cool briefly then ease wafers from sheet with a spatula.

4 Turn small molds or cups upside down and, working quickly, wrap each wafer over mold, rough-side out. Briefly hold until wafer sets, then remove to a wire rack to cool. Repeat with remaining wafers. Store in an airtight container. Spoon plum cream into cups and serve immediately.

French Christmas Pudding

serves 6–8

French Christmas Pudding

PREPARATION 20 mins   COOKING 1 hr

3 croissants, cut into

1 in/25mm slices

6 eggs, lightly beaten

1½ cups milk

1 teaspoon vanilla extract

1 teaspoon ground nutmeg

FRUIT FILLING

4 oz/125g dried figs, chopped

4 oz/125g dried dates, pitted

and chopped

½ cup orange juice

⅓ cup brandy

1 cinnamon stick

1 To make filling, place figs, dates, orange juice, brandy and cinnamon stick in a saucepan and cook over a low heat, stirring, for 15–20 minutes or until fruit is soft and mixture is thick. Remove cinnamon stick.

2 Preheat oven to 360°F/180°C and lightly butter an 4 x 8 in/11 x 21cm loaf tin. To assemble pudding, place one-third of the croissant slices in the tin. Top with half the filling. Repeat layers, ending with a layer of croissant.

3 Place eggs, milk, vanilla and nutmeg in a bowl and whisk to combine. Carefully pour egg mixture over croissant and fruit and set aside to stand for 5 minutes. Place tin in a baking dish with enough boiling water to come halfway up the sides of the tin. Cover the dish with a piece of foil. Bake for 20 minutes, then remove foil and bake for a further 20 minutes. Stand pudding in tin for 10 minutes then carefully turn out and cut into slices.

Note This dessert is best eaten warm, shortly after it is turned out.

Boiled Christmas Pudding

serves 8

Boiled Christmas Pudding

PREPARATION 4 days   COOKING 7 hrs

8 oz/250g raisins

2 oz/60g mixed peel, chopped

8 oz/250g golden raisins

4 oz/125g currants

2 oz/60g blanched almonds, chopped

3 tablespoons brandy

4 oz/250g butter

1½ cups brown sugar

zest of 1 orange

⅔ cup all-purpose flour

1 teaspoon mixed spice

½ teaspoon ground ginger

4 eggs, beaten

4 oz/125g breadcrumbs, made from stale bread

1 Place all fruits and nuts in a large bowl, sprinkle with brandy, cover and macerate overnight.

2 Cream butter until soft, add sugar and orange zest and beat until light and fluffy. Sift flour with spices, add to butter mixture alternately with eggs. Stir in breadcrumbs and fruit mixture and mix well.

3 Dip a muslin cloth into boiling water and wring out excess. Spread out flat, sprinkle center with 5 tablespoons flour and rub into cloth. Spoon pudding mixture onto center, gather up four corners firmly around mixture and mold into a round shape. Tie cloth tightly as close to mixture as possible, making a loop in the string for easy lifting.

4 Three-quarters-fill a large saucepan with water and bring to the boil. Quickly lower pudding into pan, cover and boil for 6 hours, adding more boiling water as needed. Lift pudding from pan using a wooden spoon placed through the loop, drain and suspend from a drawer or cupboard handle so that it swings freely. Allow to dry overnight or until completely cold.

5 Cut string, loosen cloth from top of pudding, remove excess flour and allow to dry completely – this takes about two days. Store pudding in an airtight container in the refrigerator. Remove pudding from refrigerator 12 hours before reheating.

6 Boil again for 1 hour then drain for 10 minutes. Remove string, peel off cloth and allow to stand for 20 minutes before cutting. Serve with warm custard.

Boiled Whiskey Fruit Cake

serves 12

Boiled Whiskey Fruit Cake

PREPARATION 30 mins   **COOKING** 1 hr 20 mins

1½ lb/750g mixed dried fruit

6 oz/180g butter

8 oz/220g brown sugar

¼ cup whiskey

3 large eggs

1¾ cup all-purpose flour

1½ teaspoons mixed spice

1½ teaspoons baking soda

¼ teaspoon salt

1¼ cups heavy cream, whipped

1 Place fruit in a saucepan, add butter, brown sugar and ¾ cup water and slowly bring to the boil. Reduce heat and simmer for 5 minutes. Remove from heat and set aside to cool until lukewarm.

2 Preheat oven to 360°F/180°C and butter and line a deep 8 in/20cm cake tin. Add whiskey to the fruit mixture, then beat in eggs, one at a time. Sift together flours, spice, baking soda and salt, add to mixture and mix well to combine.

4 Spoon into prepared tin, loosely cover with a piece of foil and bake for 50 minutes. Reduce oven temperature to 320°F/160°C and bake for 30 minutes longer or until a skewer inserted into center comes out clean.

5 Stand cake briefly in tin, then turn onto a wire rack to cool. Remove paper when cold. Serve with whipped cream.

Cherry Almond Cake

serves 12

Cherry Almond Cake

PREPARATION 1 hr   COOKING 1 hr 30 mins

11 oz/315g butter

10 oz/280g superfine sugar

2–3 drops almond extract

5 eggs

4 oz/125g glacé cherries

2 oz/60g blanched almonds, chopped

13 oz/375g all-purpose flour

1 teaspoon baking powder

⅔ cup milk

1 Preheat oven to 360°F/180°C. Butter and line a deep 8 in/20cm cake tin with baking paper.

2 Beat butter, sugar and almond extract until light and fluffy. Add eggs one at a time, beating well after each addition. Dust cherries and almonds with a little of the flour. Sift remaining flour with baking powder and add to creamed mixture alternately with the milk. Fold in cherries and almonds.

3 Place mixture in prepared tin and decorate top of cake with 6 extra cherries and extra whole almonds. Bake for 1½ hours or until cake is cooked when tested with a skewer – to prevent splitting and cracking on top, cover with 2–3 layers of baking paper for the first 30 minutes. Cool on a wire rack.

Traditional Christmas Cake

Traditional Christmas Cake

PREPARATION 12 hrs   **COOKING** 4 hrs

13 oz/375g raisins, chopped

8 oz/250g golden raisins

4 oz/125g currants

4 oz/125g glacé cherries, cut in half

4 tablespoons sherry

4 tablespoons brandy

4 oz/125g dried apricots, chopped

1 oz/30g butter

8 oz/220g soft brown sugar

zest of 1 lemon

1 tablespoon corn syrup

2 tablespoons marmalade

5 eggs

1¾ cups all-purpose flour

1 teaspoon mixed spice

1 teaspoon cinnamon

¼ teaspoon salt

4 oz/125g blanched almonds, chopped

40 almonds for decorating, optional

1 The day before baking, mix raisins, golden raisins, currants, cherries, sherry and 3 tablespoons of brandy in a bowl. Soak apricots in 2 tablespoons hot water for 1 hour, then add to fruit mixture. Cover and macerate overnight.

2 When preparing a cake tin for baking a dense fruit cake, it's necessary to use more than the usual amount of paper to line the tin – butter a deep 9 in/23cm square cake tin, then line the base and sides with a layer of buttered brown paper, then a double thickness of buttered baking paper, trimming neatly to fit into corners. Preheat oven to 300°F/150°C.

3 Beat butter, brown sugar and lemon zest until fluffy. Beat in corn syrup and marmalade. Add eggs, one at a time, beating well after each addition. If mixture curdles, stir in a tablespoon of the flour with each egg.

4 Sift together flour, spices and salt, then fold into egg mixture alternately with fruit mixture and chopped almonds. Turn into prepared tin. Decorate top with whole almonds.

5 Bake for 4 hours or until cooked when tested with a skewer. Remove from the oven and sprinkle with remaining tablespoon of brandy. Cool cake in tin. Store wrapped in a tea towel in an airtight container.

Speedy Christmas Cake

serves 12

PREPARATION 15 mins   **COOKING** 2 hrs 30 mins

8 oz/250g butter

8 oz/250g superfine sugar

zest of 1 orange

5 eggs

3 oz/90g blanched almonds, chopped

6 oz/180g golden raisins

5 oz/150g currants

5 oz/150g raisins, halved

2 oz/60g glacé cherries

1 oz/30g mixed peel, chopped

1¾ cups all-purpose flour

1 teaspoon baking powder

½ teaspoon salt

2 tablespoons orange juice

1 Preheat oven to 300°F/150°C. Butter and line a deep 8 in/20cm round cake tin.

2 Beat butter, sugar and orange zest until creamy. Beat in eggs, one at a time, and set aside. Lightly dust almonds, dried fruits and peel with a little of the flour. In a separate bowl, sift together flour, baking powder and salt. Mix in almonds, dried fruits and peel.

3 Add dry mixture to creamed mixture, then add orange juice and mix well to combine. Turn mixture into prepared tin, smooth the top and decorate with extra almonds.

4 Bake for 2½ hours or until a skewer inserted in center comes out clean. Allow to cool in tin.

We have prepared a set of special treats that can actually adorn your Christmas tree – decorated cookies and mouth-watering morsels that also work wonderfully well as little home-made gifts for your family and friends. Everyone loves the idea of edible Christmas decorations, and if you have the time to bake the whole set, you will very likely be the only person in your neighborhood sporting a tree of truly wonderful treats. But be warned – they won't last long!

Christmas Cookies

COLLECTORS EDITION

Christmas Cookies

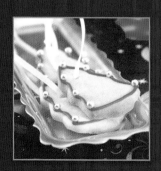

COLLECTORS EDITION

| # Russian Tea Cakes

PREPARATION 12 mins   **COOKING** 20 mins

8 oz/250g butter

½ cup superfine sugar,

plus ¼ cup

1 teaspoon vanilla extract

10 oz/280g all-purpose flour

3 oz/90g ground pecans

1 Beat together butter, ½ cup sugar and the vanilla until creamy. Add flour and pecans and mix to combine. Cover and chill until firm.

2 Preheat oven to 360°F/180°C and lightly butter 3 baking sheets. Shape dough into ¾ in/2cm balls and place on the baking sheets. Bake for 15–20 minutes or until firm and pale golden. While still hot, roll in remaining sugar. If you are planning to use them as decorations, carefully pierce them with a darning needle at this stage. Cool on wire racks.

Snowballs

makes 30

Snowballs

PREPARATION 50 mins

8 oz/250g crunchy peanut butter

2 oz/60mL vegetable oil

½ cup confectioner's sugar, sifted

6 oz/175g golden raisins, roughly chopped

3½ oz/100g sesame seeds, toasted

4 plain sweet cookies, finely crushed

4 tablespoons dried coconut

1 Stir together peanut butter and oil. Add sugar, golden raisins and sesame seeds and mix well to combine. Chill for 20 minutes. Combine crushed cookies and coconut, then shape peanut butter mixture into ¾ in/2cm balls and roll in coconut mixture. Cover and chill for a further 20 minutes until just firm, then remove from the refrigerator.

2 Using a darning needle, carefully thread ribbon through the center of the balls in sets of twos and threes.

Note Makes 30 balls, or 10 hanging treats.

Hungarian Crescents

makes 12

Hungarian Crescents

PREPARATION 40 mins **COOKING** 15 mins

1 cup all-purpose flour

½ cup almond meal

4 oz/125g butter

¼ oz/7g pack of dried yeast

2–3 tablespoons heavy cream

⅓ cup plum jelly

½ cup confectioner's sugar

1 Rub flour, almond meal and butter together with fingertips until mixture resembles coarse breadcrumbs. Combine yeast and 1 tablespoon warm water and stir to a paste. Make a well in the flour mixture and work in the yeast and cream until a soft dough forms. Allow to rest in the refrigerator for 20 minutes.

2 Preheat oven to 360°F/180°C. Roll out dough on a lightly floured surface to a thickness of ¼ in/5mm. Using a square cutter or knife , cut out 2½ in/6cm squares.

3 Place a square of rolled pastry on the work surface, and turn 45° so it looks like a diamond. Place 1 teaspoon of plum jelly in the center of the pastry. Fold pastry over filling and roll up.

4 Shape the dough into a crescent shape, and bake for 10–15 minutes or until light golden in color.

5 Cool on a cake rack. Once cooled, dust heavily with confectioner's sugar. Using a darning needle, carefully thread silver cord through the top of each crescent.

Speculaas

makes 18

Speculaas

PREPARATION 45 mins   COOKING 15 mins

2 oz/60g dark soft brown sugar

1 tablespoon milk

⅔ cup all-purpose flour, sifted

½ teaspoon ground cloves

½ teaspoon ground cinnamon

¼ teaspoon ground nutmeg

¼ teaspoon ground ginger

pinch of salt

pinch of baking powder

4 oz/125g butter, cubed

1½ tablespoons almonds, finely chopped

1½ tablespoons candied peel, finely chopped

45 whole almonds, cut in half

ICING

1½ cups confectioner's sugar

1 egg white

½ teaspoon lemon juice

1 teaspoon almond extract

1 Dissolve sugar in milk in a small saucepan over low heat, then cool. Sift together flour, spices, salt and baking powder. Rub in butter until mixture resembles breadcrumbs. Add milk mixture, almonds and peel, mix well to form a dough, then knead until pliable and no longer sticky. Wrap and chill for 30 minutes.

2 Preheat oven to 360°F/180°C and lightly butter a baking sheet. Roll out dough to ¼ in/5mm thick, then cut out star shapes. Using the circular end of a chopstick, carefully make a hole in the center of each cookie. Chill in the refrigerator for 10 minutes.

3 Bake for 5 minutes. Remove from oven and carefully make the holes with the end of the chopstick again, then return to the oven for a further 5 minutes. Cool on wire racks.

4 Sift the confectioner's sugar through a fine sieve. Using a wooden spoon in a small bowl, lightly beat the egg white. Slowly add the sugar one heaped tablespoon at a time (through the sieve again), beating thoroughly after each addition. When all of the sugar is completely mixed, add the lemon juice and almond extract and beat for another minute, then ice the cookies. Decorate each star with 5 half pieces of almond and leave to set.

5 Carefully thread a fine piece of ribbon through each cookie from behind then back through the cookie to form a loop.

Coconut Choc Balls

Coconut Choc Balls

PREPARATION 35 mins

3 oz/90g cream cheese, at room temperature

1 teaspoon vanilla extract

10 oz/300g confectioner's sugar, sifted

3 oz/90g dark chocolate, melted and slightly cooled

4 oz/125g pecans, chopped

3 oz/90g dried coconut

1 Beat together cream cheese, 1 tablespoon water and the vanilla until creamy. Gradually add confectioner's sugar, beating until blended. Stir in chocolate and nuts, then refrigerate mixture for 20 minutes.

2 Shape mixture into ¾ in/2cm balls and roll in coconut. Cover and chill for another 10 minutes until just firm. Using a darning needle, carefully thread ribbon through the center of the balls in sets of twos and threes.

Note Makes 30 balls, or 10 hanging treats.

Shortbread Angels

makes 12

Shortbread Angels

PREPARATION 20 mins   COOKING 45 mins

8 oz/250g sweet butter

3½ oz/100g superfine sugar

1 lb/500g all-purpose flour

ICING

1½ cups confectioner's sugar

1 egg white

½ teaspoon lemon juice

food coloring

silver cachous

1 Preheat oven to 360°F/180°C. Beat butter until it resembles whipped cream, then gradually add superfine sugar and continue beating until light and fluffy. Gradually mix in flour, then knead dough for 5 minutes or until very smooth.

2 Divide dough into two pieces, roll out until ¼ in/6mm thick, carefully place on baking sheets and cut into angel shapes with a cutter. Using the circular end of chopstick, carefully make a whole near the top of each cookie. Bake in center of oven for 20 minutes. Reduce oven temperature to 300°F/150°C and bake for 25 minutes longer or until golden and crisp.

3 Sift the confectioner's sugar through a fine sieve. Using a wooden spoon in a small bowl, lightly beat the egg white. Slowly add the sugar one heaped tablespoon at a time (through the sieve again), beating thoroughly after each addition. When all of the sugar is completely mixed, add the lemon juice and beat for another minute. Reserve half the icing for later use. Add 20 drops of food coloring to the remaining icing (cover with plastic wrap if not using immediately).

4 When the cookies are cool, decorate with colored icing and silver cachous.

Apricot Balls

Apricot Balls

PREPARATION 50 mins

8 oz/225g dried apricots

6½ oz/180g dried coconut

¾ cup sweetened condensed milk

1 teaspoon almond extract

100g confectioner's sugar

1 Place apricots in a food processor and process until finely chopped. Transfer to a bowl, add coconut, condensed milk and almond extract and mix to combine. Refrigerate mixture for 20 minutes, then shape into ¾ in/2cm balls and roll in confectioner's sugar. Cover and chill until firm.

2 Using a darning needle, carefully thread ribbon through the center of the balls in sets of twos and threes.

Note Makes 48 balls, or 16 hanging treats.

Zimtsterne Bells

makes 16

Zimtsterne Bells

PREPARATION 20 mins   COOKING 10 mins

7 oz/200g confectioner's sugar, sifted

7 oz/200g ground almonds

2 oz/60g sugar

squeeze of lemon juice

2 egg whites

ICING

1½ cups confectioner's sugar

1 egg white

½ teaspoon lemon juice

green food coloring

red food coloring

1 Preheat oven to 360°F/180°C. Stir together confectioner's sugar, almonds, sugar, lemon juice and egg whites to the consistency of short pastry.

2 Place dough between sheets of plastic wrap and roll out to ¼ in/5mm thick. Cut out shapes using a bell-shaped cutter. Using the circular end of a chopstick, carefully make a hole near the top of each cookies and place on paper-lined baking sheets. Bake for 5 minutes, then carefully make the holes with the end of the chopstick again and return to the oven for a further 5 minutes. Cool on wire racks.

3 To make the icing, sift the confectioner's sugar through a fine sieve. Using a wooden spoon in a small bowl, lightly beat the egg white. Slowly add the sugar one heaped tablespoon at a time (through the sieve again), beating thoroughly after each addition. When all of the sugar is completely mixed, add the lemon juice and beat for another minute.

4 Divide the icing in half and put 20 drops of green food coloring in one half and 20 drops of red food coloring in the other (cover with plastic wrap if not using immediately).

5 When cookies are cool, pipe the colored icing onto the cookies. Thread the cookies with ribbon if using as a decoration.

Christmas Butter Cookies

makes 12

Christmas Butter Cookies

PREPARATION 3 hrs 30 mins   COOKING 10 mins

13 oz/375g all-purpose flour

2 teaspoons baking powder

pinch of salt

8 oz/250g sweet butter,
cut into pieces

2 eggs

8 oz/225g superfine sugar

1½ teaspoons vanilla extract

zest of half a lemon

1 egg white, lightly beaten

plain or colored sugar
to decorate

ICING

1½ cups confectioner's sugar

1 egg white

½ teaspoon lemon juice

1 teaspoon almond extract

silver cachous

1 Sift together flour, baking powder and salt. Rub in butter with fingertips until mixture resembles breadcrumbs. Make a well in center of mixture.

2 Beat together eggs, sugar, vanilla and lemon zest, add to flour mixture and mix to make a soft dough. Knead lightly on a floured surface and cut into four pieces. Wrap each in plastic wrap and chill for 3 hours.

3 Preheat oven to 360°F/180°C and lightly butter and flour 3 baking sheets. Roll out one piece of dough at a time to ¼ in/5mm thick and cut out Christmas tree shapes. Using the circular end of a chopstick, carefully make a hole near the top of each cookie. Place cookies in the refrigerator for 10 minutes.

4 Brush with egg white and bake for 5 minutes. Carefully re-make the holes with the end of the chopstick and return to the oven for a further 5 minutes. Cool on wire racks.

5 Sift the confectioner's sugar through a fine sieve. Using a wooden spoon in a small bowl, lightly beat the egg white. Slowly add the sugar one heaped tablespoon at a time (through the sieve again), beating thoroughly after each addition. When all of the sugar is completely mixed, add the lemon juice and almond extract and beat for another minute (cover with plastic wrap if not using immediately). Pipe the icing onto the cookies and decorate with silver cachous.

Ginger Spice Cookies

Ginger Spice Cookies

PREPARATION 45 mins   **COOKING** 10 mins

4 oz/125g butter

½ cup firmly packed brown sugar

½ cup corn syrup

1 egg yolk

2 cups all-purpose flour

2 teaspoons ground ginger

1 teaspoon mixed spice

1 teaspoon baking soda

good pinch of ground cinnamon

ICING

1 cup confectioner's sugar

1 egg white

few drops of lemon juice

food coloring

silver cachous

1 Preheat oven to 360°F/180°C and lightly butter 2 baking trays. In a mixing bowl, cream the butter and sugar until light and creamy. Beat in the corn syrup and egg yolk.

2 Sift the dry ingredients together and stir into the mixture in two batches. Turn onto a floured board and knead lightly. Wrap the dough in plastic wrap and chill for 30 minutes.

3 Roll out to ¼ in/5mm thick on a floured surface and cut into decorative Christmas shapes. Using the circular end of a chopstick, carefully make a hole in each cookie. Transfer to the baking trays and bake for 5 minutes. Re-make the holes with the chopstick and return to the oven for another 5 minutes. Cool on wire racks.

4 To make the icing, sift the confectioner's sugar through a fine sieve. Using a wooden spoon in a small bowl, lightly beat the egg white. Slowly add the sugar one heaped tablespoon at a time, beating thoroughly after each addition. When all of the sugar is completely mixed, add the lemon juice and beat for another minute.

5 Divide the icing in 3. In one third, place about 15 drops of food coloring. In another third, place about 15 drops of a different food coloring. Leave the final third white. Ice one-third of the cookies in each color, and decorate with silver cachous.

6 Leave cookies to dry, then thread loops of ribbon or silver cord through the holes.

Almond-Crusted Tea Cookies

makes 18

PREPARATION 1 hr 20 mins   COOKING 20 mins

1 Cream the butter, sugar and almond extract until light and fluffy, then beat in the eggs. Sift the flour and baking powder together and fold into the butter mixture. Form into a ball, cover with plastic wrap and refrigerate for 1 hour.

2 To make the topping, chop the blanched almonds until fine and even but still a little chunky – do not use a food processor. Combine with the sugar in a wide bowl.

3 Roll out the dough on a lightly floured surface to a thickness of ⅓ in/1cm. Cut out rounds with a 3 in/8cm cookie cutter, then use a 25mm cutter to cut a hole out of the center of each round. Re-roll the off-cuts and repeat as before until all the dough is used.

4 Preheat oven to 360°F/180°C and lightly butter an oven tray or line with baking paper. Mix the egg yolk with 1 teaspoon water to make an egg wash. Brush the top of each cookie with egg wash and sprinkle thickly with the almond sugar mixture. Lightly press the almond sugar onto the cookies, then place onto the oven tray. Bake for 15–20 minutes until golden brown and firm. Cool on the oven tray.

8 oz/250g butter

4 oz/125g superfine sugar

1 teaspoon almond extract

2 eggs

1 lb/450g all-purpose flour

½ teaspoon baking powder

1 egg yolk

TOPPING

3½ oz/100g blanched almonds

2 oz/60g superfine sugar

Note To use as decorations, simply tie tinsel loops around cookies bundled together in sets of two.

From fruit punch to egg-nog to colourful mixed drinks and cocktails, we start with some child-friendly Christmas favorites then move on to provide some parent-friendly cheer. Rounding out this chapter are some lavish show-stoppers that may leave you quietly thankful this season of excess only comes once a year!

Christmas Drinks

COLLECTORS EDITION

Christmas Drinks

COLLECTORS EDITION

PREPARATION 5 mins

2 cups apple juice

4 cups cranberry juice

1½ cups lime cordial

2 tablespoons sugar

1 Combine all ingredients with 2 cups water in a large jug. Add a large block of ice to keep punch cool.

serves 1

Shirley Temple

PREPARATION 5 mins

1 oz/30mL grenadine

3 oz/90mL pineapple juice

5 oz/150mL lemonade

1 tablespoon passionfruit pulp

wedge of pineapple

1 cherry

1 Pour the grenadine and pineapple juice into a tall glass. Add the lemonade, then the passionfruit pulp. Garnish with the pineapple wedge and cherry.

Milk-Nog

Milk-Nog

PREPARATION 5 mins

1 egg

7 oz/200mL milk

1 oz/30mL sugar syrup

2 drops vanilla extract

ground cinnamon

1 Combine egg, milk, sugar syrup and vanilla in a shaker with ice. Shake well and strain into a 10 oz/300mL highball glass. Top with a dusting of cinnamon.

Champagne Cocktail

Champagne Cocktail

PREPARATION 3 mins

1 sugar cube

6 drops Angostura bitters

½ oz/15mL Cognac or brandy

5 oz/150mL Champagne or sparkling white wine

1 red cherry

1 In a Champagne flute, soak the sugar cube in the bitters for 20 seconds, then add brandy. Top with Champagne or sparkling white wine, and garnish with the cherry.

Tall Dutch Egg-Nog

Tall Dutch Egg-Nog

PREPARATION 5 mins

1 oz/30mL white rum

1 oz/30mL orange juice

2 teaspoons dark rum

2 teaspoons advocaat

4 oz/125mL milk

1 egg yolk

ground cinnamon

1 Combine the white rum, orange juice, dark rum, advocaat, milk and egg yolk with ice in a shaker. Shake well, then strain into a 10 oz/285mL beer glass. Top with a sprinkle of cinnamon.

Brandy Crusta

PREPARATION 5 mins

2 oz/60g sugar

1 slice of lemon

3 oz/90mL brandy

1 dash Angostura bitters

3 dashes maraschino liqueur

1 maraschino cherry

1 Tip the sugar onto a small plate or saucer. Run the slice of lemon around the edge of a stemmed glass, then dip the glass in the sugar.

2 Combine brandy, bitters and maraschino liqueur in a shaker. Shake, then strain into the glass, being careful not to remove the sugar from the rim. Garnish with the cherry.

Hot Whiskey Toddy

Hot Whiskey Toddy

PREPARATION 5 mins

1 lemon

1 clove

2 sugar cubes

2 oz/60mL Irish whiskey

1 Cut a piece of rind from the lemon and push the clove through it. Cut a slice off the lemon.

2 Place sugar cubes in the bottom of a glass, add the lemon slice and clove-studded rind. Add the whiskey, then top up with hot water. Serve while warm.

Long Island Iced Tea

Long Island Iced Tea

PREPARATION 5 mins

1 oz/30mL vodka

1 oz/30mL lemon juice

1 oz/30mL tequila

1 oz/30mL sugar syrup

1 oz/30mL white rum

dash of cola

1 oz/30mL Cointreau

twist of lemon

fresh mint leaves

1 Place ice in a 10 oz/285mL highball glass, then pour over vodka, lemon juice, tequila, sugar syrup, white rum, cola and Cointreau. Garnish with lemon and mint, and serve with a straw.

Candy Cane

Candy Cane

PREPARATION 5 mins

½ oz/15mL grenadine

½ oz/15mL crème de menthe

1 oz/30mL vodka

1 In a tall Dutch cordial glass, pour in the grenadine. Then, over the back of a teaspoon, carefully pour in the crème de menthe, then the vodka. Drink in one shot.

serves 1

Strawberry Cream

PREPARATION 5 mins

⅔ oz/20mL strawberry liqueur

⅓ oz/10mL heavy cream

1 In an embassy glass, carefully pour in the strawberry liqueur, then pour in the cream slowly over the back of a teaspoon.
Drink in 1 shot.

Note Make in small batches up to 20 minutes ahead of your party if you wish.

After Eight

serves 1

After Eight

PREPARATION 2 mins

½ oz/15mL Kahlúa

⅓ oz/10mL crème de menthe

⅔ oz/20mL Irish cream liqueur

twist of lemon peel

1 In a 2 oz/60mL fancy shooter glass, carefully pour in the Kahlúa, then add the crème de menthe slowly over the back of a teaspoon, then pour in the Irish cream also over the teaspoon. Garnish with the lemon peel and serve.

Index

We are proud to present the **COLLECTORS EDITION** series of books as a suite of our favorite and most asked for recipes.

This series is bound together in a premium collectable format that can be added to the recipe section of your bookshelf.

Watch out for the following titles, start collecting, continue cooking, and finally, enjoy the end results of a beautifully prepared meal.

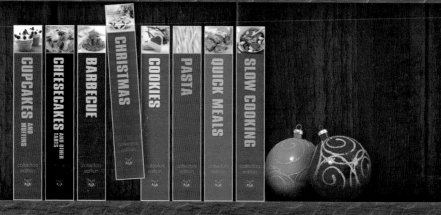